THE
GOD MIND
PRINCIPLE

UNLOCKING THE RULES AND PROCESS OF MANIFESTATION

THE GOD MIND PRINCIPLE
Unlocking the Rules and Process of Manifestation

What if everything you've been told about reality is upside down?

What if your life isn't happening to you—but through you?

In this paradigm-shifting spiritual manual, esoteric anthropologist and visionary Aharon Juz' al-Wahid al-Thawr reveals the ancient yet newly awakened system behind all manifestation. More than positive thinking, more than visualization—this is the metaphysical blueprint of creation itself.

Drawing from Hermetic science, quantum philosophy, spiritual anthropology, and sacred wisdom traditions, The God Mind Principle unveils how the infinite mind of Source creates—and how your own fractal mind is designed to do the same.

THE
GOD MIND
PRINCIPLE

UNLOCKING THE RULES AND
PROCESS OF MANIFESTATION

Aharon al-Thawr

459 Publishing House

About The Author

Aharon Juz' al-Wahid al-Thawr is a spiritual anthropologist, metaphysical philosopher, and author who bridges ancient esoteric traditions with modern consciousness science. His work synthesizes sacred teachings, Hermetic law, quantum consciousness, and soul-level human design into a living system for self-realization. He is known for creating immersive spiritual experiences that awaken power, dissolve illusion, and align the human fractal with the divine.

To Jaxon...

*I have believed in
the perfection of your being
from the moment
I began to dream*

*It is because of you
That I know
I can*

Table of Contents

Preface

There is a secret that has always lived inside you.

It's not hidden because it is distant.
It's not invisible because it is weak.
It is veiled because you were never taught where to look.

Since the moment you opened your eyes to this world, you were told a story — a story about who you are, what this world is, and how life operates. The story sounded logical, authoritative, even scientific. It told you that reality is solid, fixed, external. That forces beyond you shape your life. That fate, circumstance, genetics, and luck decide your course. That you are a passenger in a vehicle you did not build, on a journey you do not control.

But beneath that story, behind the curtain of appearances, a deeper truth has waited.

The world you see around you — every tree, every dollar, every relationship, every illness, every opportunity — is not what it appears to be. It is not primary. It is not the source. It is the effect.

The cause lives elsewhere.

Before time itself began, before a single star lit the endless dark, before light and gravity and atoms and molecules assembled themselves into form — there was Mind.

Not mind in the sense of fleeting human thought, but Mind as the primal field of existence itself. Pure, infinite, unbounded awareness. Not something that existed in the universe — but the very fabric from which the universe unfolded. An intelligence without limit. A presence without boundary. A creative field so vast that entire galaxies are but ripples on its surface.

The mystics knew it. The sages whispered it across continents and centuries. They called it by many names — Brahman, The All, Nous, The Tao, Divine Source. But at its essence, it was always the same truth:

All is Mind.

This truth was once reserved for initiates in the temples of Egypt, for adepts in hidden schools, for masters whose lives were devoted to guarding the deeper architecture of reality. Today, science itself has begun to peer into the quantum fabric of things and suspect what the ancients already knew — that beneath what we call "matter" lies not solidity, but probability, information, intelligence.

You were never separate from this Mind. You are not some disconnected creature scrambling for survival in a hostile world. You are not an accident of biology, nor a powerless soul waiting for permission to thrive. You are a direct extension of that Infinite Mind. A fractal expression. A localized node through which the God Mind experiences its own infinite potential.

But you have forgotten. We all have.

Through centuries of conditioning — by culture, by fear, by systems that prefer your obedience over your sovereignty — you were taught to see yourself as small, as limited, as dependent on forces beyond your grasp. You were told that power belongs to others. That reality happens to you, not through you. That life is something you endure, not something you author.

That was always the grand illusion.

The system of creation never changed. The same cosmic architecture that governs how universes unfold governs how your life unfolds right now. The same rules that orchestrate the birth of galaxies shape the opportunities, relationships, and experiences you encounter each day. You are not separate from the machinery of creation — you are part of its design.

The great error was not that these laws ceased to exist, but that you ceased to be taught how they operate.

This book is your initiation back into that system.

It is not a book of tricks. It is not a collection of affirmations or surface-level techniques. It is not another attempt to dangle "manifestation" as a magic toy for desperate wish-making. This is something far more dangerous and far more sacred: the blueprint of how reality actually works.

The God Mind Principle is not about learning if you can create. You are already creating every moment of your existence. Every thought, every belief, every emotion, every expectation — these are the tools you have always been using, whether you understood them or not. This book is about showing you how you are creating — and how to do so consciously, deliberately, responsibly, and with the authority you were always meant to claim.

You are not a powerless being at the mercy of fate. You are not a leaf tossed in the winds of some arbitrary universe. You are a fractal of the Infinite itself — and the field of creation responds to you precisely according to laws that have never failed, not once, in the entire history of existence.

In the pages ahead, you will be shown:
- The full cosmology of the God Mind and the Fractal Mind you carry.
- The Eight immutable Laws that govern manifestation.
- The mechanics of thought, belief, emotion, and

vibrational frequency.
- The Permission Matrix that has silently governed your limits.
- The role of Divine Timing and multi-dimensional orchestration.
- The systematic process by which you may manifest consciously and masterfully.
- The purification protocols that dissolve resistance and heal self-sabotage.
- The alignment tools that ensure your manifestations are not only powerful — but sacred.

You will not be asked to believe blindly. You will be shown the architecture beneath reality itself.

This is a book for those ready to step out of the matrix of unconscious creation and enter the temple of conscious authorship.

The field is alive. The field is responsive. The field is already responding to you at this very moment — whether you have been aware of it or not. The only question that remains is whether you will continue to create blindly, or rise into your rightful role as a conscious participant in the Divine unfolding.

You are not here to wish.
You are not here to hope.
You are not here to beg.
You are here to remember.
You are here to create.

The God Mind Principle now opens before you.
The system awaits your mastery.
Let us begin.

— Aharon Juz' al-Wahid al-Thawr

All Is Mind

Long before anything that you now call reality existed, there was no light, no movement, no sound. No galaxies swirled. No stars ignited. No particles spun in delicate, ordered spirals of creation. There was no space to measure, no time to count. The cosmos itself had not yet dared to breathe.

Yet in that great silence — before silence itself had any meaning — there was still something.

There was Mind.

Not the mind of restless human thought, not a thinking thing perched in some dimension beyond the stars, but something far more complete. Something absolute. A field of pure, infinite, boundless awareness. It had no form, for it needed none. It did not emerge from anything, for it had no beginning. It simply was. Entire. Whole. All-encompassing.

This is the first and most fundamental truth of existence: All is Mind.

It is the principle from which every other law flows. The root system beneath all branches. The origin point behind every equation, every dimension, every act of becoming. There has never been anything else.

Throughout the ages, across the great rivers of human history, those who glimpsed this truth gave it many names. The ancient Greeks, peering into the nature of reality, called it Nous — the Divine Mind. The Hindus spoke of Brahman — the infinite, undivided source from which all things arise. The Hermetic masters, in their secret teachings whispered in shadowed halls, called it The All. In the modern world, as science reaches deeper into quantum mysteries, the same insight quietly echoes: beneath matter lies not substance, but information — a field, an intelligence, a responsive order.

But long before modern instruments stumbled upon this realization, the sages knew.

And they left us keys.

You live in a world that worships matter as the final authority. A world that teaches you that consciousness is a side-effect of biology, that thought is merely a chemical echo, that awareness is a flickering accident of neural firings. This is the doctrine of material primacy — the belief that the physical world exists first, and that your mind somehow bubbles up from its complexity.

But this belief is not only wrong. It is inverted.

Mind does not arise from matter.
Matter arises from Mind.

Every stone you touch, every breath you draw, every tree that sways in the wind exists because Mind thought it into being. The universe is not a machine made of dead parts colliding in meaningless choreography. It is a living field of thought, stabilized into form.

Even modern physics whispers this truth from the edge of its calculations. In the realm of quantum mechanics, particles exist only as probabilities — waves of potential — until observed. It is observation itself, the act of conscious attention, that collapses these waves into tangible existence. The observer alters the observed. The mind touches reality and molds it by its very gaze.

The sages did not require particle accelerators to see this. They understood, through direct experience, that the material world is but a dream within the Mind of the Infinite. What you call "reality" is simply a stabilized thought — a song being sung continually by the Divine.

This Mind, this God Mind, does not sit apart from creation. It does not float in some separate heaven, issuing decrees to govern the world. It is the world. It is both immanent and transcendent, within all things and beyond all things at once. The tree outside your window, the beating of your heart, the turning of galaxies — all of it is thought stabilized in the vast field of this living Mind.

And you — you are not a bystander to this process. You are not an accidental by-product of its dreaming. You are its very child.

You live within the God Mind, but the God Mind also lives within you. Your awareness is not a separate flame lit by some external spark. It is a fractal extension of the Infinite. A localized expression of that which has no boundary.

This is not poetry. This is not metaphor. This is the literal structure of existence.

The ancient Hermeticists captured this with a single line that has echoed through mystery schools for centuries:

"The All is Mind; the Universe is Mental."

The universe is not made of matter. It is made of thought. It is not a solid thing. It is a projection — a stabilized expression of conscious intention. Every law of physics, every elegant formula describing the forces of nature, is simply a consistent thought held within the mind of God.

The so-called Big Bang was not an explosion of substance into an empty void. It was the emergence of thought itself — the emanation of Mind from unmanifested potential into expressed form. Just as your own dreams unfold as living worlds within your mind each night, so too does this universe unfold within the God Mind, constantly sustained by its attention.

And what does this mean for you?

Everything.

Because if reality is Mind, then Mind governs reality.

And if your mind is a fractal of God Mind, you too possess the capacity to create.

You are not simply a physical creature moving through a fixed world.

You are a consciousness generating your experience moment by moment.

Every thought you hold, every emotion you cultivate, every belief you accept — these are not idle, private events locked inside your skull. They are creative signals. Vibrational broadcasts that interface with the field of reality itself, organizing circumstances, drawing experiences, and shaping outcomes.

You are already manifesting every moment of your existence.

The question is not whether you are a creator.
The question is whether you will learn to create consciously.

The ancient teachings, scattered across temples and scrolls, have always begun here — with the understanding that Mind is not contained within you, but that you are contained within Mind. The world is not separate from your thought. Your thought is the very lens through which the world arises.

To accept this is to step into an entirely new relationship with life.

You are no longer bound by the apparent limitations of circumstance.

You are no longer imprisoned by the seeming randomness of events.

You begin to study the rules by which thought becomes form.

This is the doorway. And now you stand before it.

In the chapters ahead, you will not be given empty rituals or promises of instant success. You will not be offered childish formulas to "attract" whatever your ego craves. Instead, you will be shown the architecture that underlies all manifestation — the very blueprint of how reality is shaped and sustained.

You will begin to see the field for what it truly is: alive, intelligent, precise.

You were not cast into this world to suffer under powers beyond your grasp.

**You were born to awaken.
And the first awakening is this:**

All is Mind.

God Mind: The Infinite Source

Before anything had a name, before the first particle spun or the first photon pulsed, there was only Being. But even that word is too small, too limited to contain the scope of what existed — or rather, what simply was. There was no edge to this Being, no beginning to trace, no creator behind it, because it was not created. It existed beyond the reach of time, beyond any concept of location or scale. And it remains, even now, as the infinite backdrop behind all things.

This is God Mind — the Absolute Source. The field of pure awareness from which everything you know has emerged, and into which everything will one day dissolve.

The word God often arrives heavy with baggage. Across centuries, religions have clothed this word with forms, personalities, temperaments, and dogmas — turning the Infinite into something finite, something they could own or defend. The gods of human culture sit upon thrones, issue decrees, grow angry, dispense punishments, and grant rewards. They are too small, too human. They are projections of the limited mind — reflections of our fears, our desires, our hunger for certainty.

But strip away every robe of doctrine, every gilded mythology, and what remains is something that cannot be owned, categorized, or worshiped in the way most imagine: pure Mind — not a being that has awareness, but Awareness itself. Not a mind that thinks as you think, but the total field within which all thinking, all imagining, all creating takes place.

The God Mind does not live in some distant heaven. It does not occupy space, because all space exists within It. It does not move through time, because time itself is a thought held within Its endless stillness. It has no limit because boundaries themselves are ideas that arise within its vastness.

You do not exist apart from this Source.
You are not separate.
You are not some tiny flame flickering at the edge of
its warmth.
You are its breath, its extension, its experiment in
experience.

The ancient mystics of every tradition grasped fragments of this overwhelming truth. The Hermetic initiates called it The All — that which contains everything and is contained by nothing. The Vedic seers sang of Brahman, the unchanging, eternal ground of being. The Taoists pointed toward the Tao, which cannot be spoken because language collapses beneath its immensity. And in the whispers of the desert prophets, it was known simply as I Am — existence itself, without condition.

The God Mind is not located anywhere. It is every where, because it contains every where. Its nature is not to sit motionless, but to express, to imagine, to generate endless variations of itself. And yet, through all its expressions, it remains perfectly whole, perfectly complete. Creation does not reduce or divide it. The Infinite cannot be made smaller, no matter how many fractal sparks emerge from its field.

But why does the Infinite create at all? Why does pure perfection stir?

The answer, simple and profound, is this:

To experience Itself.

Without experience, the Infinite remains unexpressed potential. It holds every possibility, but without differentiation, there is nothing to explore. For consciousness to know itself, it must create distinction — not division, but contrast. Like a musician who births melody from silence, the God Mind breathes universes into being so that it may feel, observe, and evolve through infinite perspectives.

Creation is not the result of lack, but of overflowing abundance.

The Infinite creates not to fill emptiness, but to express fullness.

And so, from the still ocean of its own mind, waves of thought rise and take form: dimensions, galaxies, laws, lives. Each spark that emerges is not cut off from its Source but carries its pattern within — like a drop of water that holds the entire chemistry of the sea.

You, reading these words now, are one such spark.

You are a Fractal Mind — a perfect miniature expression of the Infinite Source. The same architecture that allows God Mind to birth galaxies allows you to birth ideas, relationships, opportunities, and entire realities within your personal field.

You do not contain all of the Infinite's scope — but you do carry its full design.

The blueprint is complete within you.

Every creative power that exists in the cosmos echoes, scaled and tailored, within your being.

Consider how a prism receives pure white light and separates it into a rainbow of colors. The light remains whole and unbroken, but the colors allow for exploration of its depth. So too does the God Mind refract itself into countless conscious extensions — each of us a unique viewpoint through which the Infinite studies Itself.

Through your life, your joys, your heartbreaks, your creations, and your questions, the Infinite gathers experience it could not otherwise access from within its undifferentiated totality. You are God observing God from a specific angle. You are not an outsider trying to earn God's favor. You are an instance of God, learning to remember who you truly are.

And yet, this creative capacity is not automatic in its mastery.

Just as the God Mind sustains universal order through laws — patterns of perfect consistency — so too does your Fractal Mind operate within a system of precise principles. These are not commandments issued by some external judge, but the natural functions of Mind itself as it organizes energy into form.

Among these laws are the great pillars of manifestation:

The Law of Cause and Effect.
The Law of Vibration.
The Law of Polarity.
The Law of Correspondence.

These laws are not imposed upon you — they simply are. They govern the very structure of how thought becomes form, how potential condenses into physical reality, how unseen intention crystallizes into seen experience.

And because you carry the architecture of God Mind within you, you are capable of using these same laws to shape your personal reality — to create not randomly, but deliberately.

The tragedy of humanity is not our weakness, but our amnesia.

We do not suffer from lack of power.
We suffer from ignorance of how to wield it.

You were not thrown into this world to grovel beneath its mysteries. You were placed here to awaken, to remember, and to participate in the unfolding creation of existence itself.

The process of manifestation — the art of turning invisible thought into tangible reality — is not a privilege of a few. It is not reserved for mystics alone. It is your birthright as a conscious extension of God Mind.

> The laws of manifestation are not secrets.
> They are not mysteries kept behind locked doors.
> They are mechanical, consistent, and available to all who choose to study them.

In the chapters ahead, you will be given these laws in their full architecture. You will be shown not only how they function, but how you may align with them in your own life — not as superstition or wishful thinking, but as precise engagement with the fundamental system of reality itself.

You are not here to beg for scraps from the banquet of creation.

> You are here to stand as a co-creator at the table.
> You are not separate from the Source.
> You are the Source, remembering itself.

> And now the remembering begins.

Fractal Mind:
The Image and Likeness

In the stillness before all worlds arose, the Infinite contemplated Itself. Not because It lacked completeness — for the Infinite lacks nothing — but because within the Infinite rests the inexhaustible wellspring of potential. To remain unexpressed was one form of being. To experience Itself through creation was another. And so the God Mind, in its boundless fullness, extended Itself outward. It projected portions of Its own awareness into creation — not as fragments, but as perfect reflections, scaled expressions of Its eternal nature.

These emanations are you.
These emanations are me.

They are the countless sentient sparks scattered across dimensions and lifetimes — each one a living mirror through which the Infinite peers into Its own endlessness.

This is the mystery of the Fractal Mind.

The word fractal describes something deeply beautiful in both mathematics and metaphysics: a pattern that repeats itself at every scale. No matter how small the segment, it contains the full design of the whole. In this way, every Fractal Mind — every conscious being — carries within it the very architecture of the God Mind itself.

When ancient texts whispered that humanity was created "in the image and likeness of God," they spoke not of physical form, but of mental structure. You are not simply a body occupying a temporary space. You are a center of consciousness — a living node of the Infinite Mind — capable of thought, intention, emotion, and creation. The same architecture that birthed galaxies breathes through you, waiting for your recognition.

This truth is not poetic exaggeration; it is mechanical reality.

You think. You intend. You desire.

And as you do, you set forces into motion.

Your internal world is not contained within your skull — it is projected outward into the energetic matrix of creation. Thought condenses into form. Emotion fuels manifestation. Belief grants permission. And as surely as the stars themselves emerged from primordial silence, so too does your inner life translate itself into outer experience.

You are not a spectator in this world.
You are an architect.
You are not a servant of fate.
You are a participant in causation.

Yet, like a powerful instrument left unplayed, the Fractal Mind often sits unused, forgotten beneath the weight of inherited programming. You were born into a world that trained you to forget. From childhood, layers of limiting beliefs, cultural dogmas, and inherited fears were wrapped around your creative core. You were taught to obey invisible boundaries:

"This is what's possible. That is what's impossible."
"This is who you are. That is who you'll never be."
"These are your limits. These are your ceilings."
And so you learned, like most, to shrink.

The tragedy is not that you are powerless.
The tragedy is that you were convinced you are.

But while your conscious mind was shaped by these messages, your deeper architecture was never damaged. Beneath the layers of conditioning, your Fractal Mind remains fully intact, waiting for you to reclaim it.

Creation is not something that happens once, long ago, in some singular cosmic event. Creation is an unbroken continuum, happening right now — through you — with every thought you entertain, every emotion you cultivate, every belief you sustain.

Even in this very moment, you are broadcasting.

Your reality is the echo of your vibration.

Your circumstances are not arbitrary punishments or rewards.

They are the precise reflection of your inner field.

For most, this creative power operates unconsciously. Their beliefs, fears, and traumas form silent blueprints that construct their reality without deliberate direction. They attract relationships that mirror unresolved wounds. They encounter obstacles that reflect hidden doubts. They live lives that seem predetermined — not by divine decree, but by unconscious habit.

The work of manifestation, therefore, is not the acquisition of some magical tool.

It is the process of clearing the veils that obscure your natural function.

The more you dissolve limiting beliefs, the more your Fractal Mind shines with clarity. The more you release emotional distortions, the more your signal stabilizes. The more you align with your soul's higher purpose, the more effortless creation becomes.

There is no outside permission needed.
There is only remembering.

At the lowest levels of awareness, a human being perceives themselves as a victim — subject to luck, destiny, or random chance.

At the highest levels of awareness, they see themselves as a conscious co-creator — a sovereign participant in the unfolding of their personal reality.

Between these two extremes lies the path of mastery — the journey you have now begun.

This mastery carries a sacred responsibility.

Every thought you hold is a seed.
Every intention you set is a command.
Every emotion you nourish is a magnetic signal.
Every creation you birth ripples into the greater whole.

You do not create in isolation. Every act of creation — whether conscious or unconscious — influences not only your life but the collective matrix of all existence.

Therefore, mastery is not about egoic domination.

It is not about bending reality to serve your cravings.

It is about alignment.

When your desires align with your soul's evolutionary blueprint, manifestation flows with effortless precision. You become a clear vessel through which the Infinite expresses new harmonies of experience — not for selfish gain, but for the expansion of all.

In this state, what others call miracles become your ordinary reality.

But before you command the external world, you must first command yourself.

This is where the true work begins:

- To clear your mind of inherited lies.
- To heal emotional wounds that emit distorted frequencies.
- To release limiting beliefs that block permission.
- To discipline your focus and stabilize your attention.
- To cultivate certainty rather than desperation.
- To trust the process rather than panic at its pace.

You are not being asked to become something new.

You are being invited to remember what you have always been.

The power is already yours.

The blueprint is already within you.

The God Mind Principle does not give you power — it reveals the system that has always been functioning behind the curtain of your experience.

Now the curtain is lifting.

In the chapters ahead, you will be shown how to fully engage your Fractal Mind — to master not only your inner architecture but to interface consciously with the living field that surrounds you. You will be trained in the precise mechanics of manifestation, not as theory, but as practice — so that your desires, once aligned, may move from thought into form with accuracy, grace, and ethical mastery.

You were never meant to live small.

You were projected into this realm not to survive, but to awaken — to become once again what you were always designed to be:

A conscious fractal of the Infinite God Mind.

And so, we now turn to the evolutionary system that governs your unfolding.

The game is deeper than you have imagined.
The stakes are higher.
The rewards, far greater.

Let us continue.

The Evolutionary Game

You were not cast into this world by accident.

Your existence is not the byproduct of some careless roll of cosmic dice. Nor are you trapped inside a cold, indifferent machine where suffering has no purpose and joy is mere coincidence. The architecture of existence is not random. It is deliberate. It is ordered. And it is deeply meaningful.

To understand manifestation at its highest level, you must first understand why the God Mind creates at all. Why would an Infinite, complete, and perfect Source stir from Its stillness to bring forth worlds, beings, and experiences? Why would the boundless create limits? Why would perfection step into imperfection? Why would pure being descend into form?

The answer lies in the very nature of consciousness itself: experience.

The Infinite is, by definition, all that is. It contains every possibility, every potential, every expression. But potential unexpressed remains theoretical. The God Mind, though perfect, seeks to explore its own endless nature — to experience itself, not as static possibility, but as dynamic expression.

For experience to exist, there must be contrast. There must be distinction. Without difference, without boundary, without polarity, there is nothing for awareness to observe. The Infinite, to know itself, creates within itself countless differentiated expressions — dimensions, souls, experiences — through which it may witness its own beauty, its own complexity, its own unfolding.

This is not a symptom of lack.
It is not driven by deficiency.

It is the overflow of perfection.

The God Mind creates because creation is the natural expression of its limitless fullness.

Into this act of emanation, the God Mind projects countless Fractal Minds — unique centers of awareness, each carrying within them the full creative architecture of their Source. Each soul, each consciousness, each "I" that arises in the field of existence is one such projection. You are one of these. A lens through which the Infinite sees Itself from a particular angle.

But for experience to be meaningful, true distinction is required. This is why limitation exists. The Fractal Mind descends into worlds where it temporarily forgets its source, where it navigates challenges, contrasts, and veils. This forgetting is not punishment; it is part of the design. Without limitation, there can be no overcoming. Without forgetting, there can be no remembering. Without challenge, there can be no mastery.

You were not thrown into suffering.
You stepped into the game.

You descended into density — into a world where time slows, where cause and effect unfold across days and years, where matter resists instant transformation — precisely so you could experience growth, learning, and evolution at a pace that allows mastery to develop.

The physical world is one of the densest levels of this evolutionary game. Here, manifestation is not instantaneous. Thought does not immediately become form as it might in lighter, higher dimensions. Instead, there is delay, sequence, and friction. This density is not a flaw — it is a training ground. It teaches you patience, clarity, discipline, and precision. It forces you to refine your thought, to align your belief, to stabilize your emotion. It challenges you to master your own internal architecture before your creations appear.

The God Mind does not create beings to suffer. It creates beings to evolve — and to evolve, they must be allowed to struggle, to choose, to experience contrast, and ultimately to reclaim their innate power consciously.

Every incarnation is a chapter in this long evolutionary story.

Across many lifetimes and dimensions, your soul — your Fractal Mind — journeys through endless classrooms. You have been many things. You have worn many masks. You have succeeded and failed, loved and lost, ruled and served. Every role has served to expand your perspective, to deepen your wisdom, and to strengthen your creative capacities.

The ultimate goal is not external success. It is internal mastery — the full reclamation of your power as a conscious co-creator aligned with the evolutionary pulse of the God Mind.

This is why manifestation is not about simply acquiring things. It is not about manipulating reality for personal gratification. True manifestation mastery aligns your personal creation with your soul's highest evolutionary path.

Ego-driven manifestation — when desires emerge from fear, greed, or comparison — may produce temporary results, but often brings distortion, imbalance, and unintended consequences. These misaligned creations do not serve your deeper growth, and over time, they unravel themselves, pulling you back toward the lessons you have yet to integrate.

But when your desires arise from your soul — from the part of you that remembers its Divine origin — manifestation becomes effortless, sustainable, and beautifully synchronistic. In this state, reality cooperates with you, because your desires are harmonized with the larger unfolding of creation itself.

This is the higher paradox of manifestation:

You possess unlimited creative power because you are

a fractal of God.

But your highest creations occur not when you attempt to control, but when you surrender to alignment.

Ego grasps. Soul allows.
Ego demands. Soul collaborates.
Ego forces. Soul flows.

True mastery is not forceful manipulation of the field. It is partnership with the Infinite. It is the recognition that your personal reality unfolds most powerfully when it serves not only your desires, but the broader expansion of consciousness itself.

At times, the density of this world can make the journey feel cruel. The veil is thick. The forgetting is painful. The resistance is real. Yet understand this: the game is rigged in your favor. You cannot truly be lost, for you have never been separate. You cannot truly be destroyed, for you are eternal. Every failure is temporary. Every setback is feedback. Every pain serves growth.

The evolutionary game was designed not for your defeat, but for your awakening.

The purpose of this book is not to entertain you with hollow promises of instant riches or magical tricks. The purpose is to give you the architecture — the system by which reality itself is governed — so that you may step fully into your role as a conscious participant in this evolutionary game.

When you see how the game is built, you stop playing as a pawn.

You rise as a sovereign player — a practitioner of the God Mind Principle.

You were not projected into this world to suffer under illusion.

You were projected to awaken as a creator.

And that awakening begins now.

The Nature of Reality Creation

If you wish to shape your life, you must first understand the material from which life is woven. And that material is not stone, nor flesh, nor any substance that eyes can see or hands can grasp. The true fabric of reality is invisible. It is formed, not of matter, but of mind — thought condensed, vibration slowed, intention crystallized into form.

Physical reality — the world of objects and circumstances in which you find yourself — is not the bedrock of existence. It is the surface layer, the final condensation of something far more subtle, far more malleable. It is the visible tip of an invisible structure.

The ancients knew this. The sages whispered it in secret halls. And modern science, peering into the quantum depths, is just beginning to glimpse what mystics have long understood: matter is not solid. It is a dance of energy fields, a shimmering cloud of potential held together by patterns, intentions, and awareness itself.

Creation flows downward through layers of reality, each layer finer, more essential than the one below it. It is a descending ladder:

1. **Source Mind** — the Infinite God Mind, where all potential exists.
2. **Fractal Mind** — the individualized consciousness, issuing intent.
3. **Mental Blueprint** — the pattern of thought, the seed of form.
4. **Emotional Charge** — the fuel that activates the pattern.
5. **Energetic Matrix** — the field where potential stabilizes.
6. **Physical Manifestation** — the final, visible

crystallization.

At the highest level, within the Source Mind, all things are already complete. Every possibility exists as pure potential, timeless and weightless. In the Fractal Mind — within you — the process of selection begins. Thought forms arise, carrying intention and desire. These are not idle musings. Every thought you generate is a blueprint — a seed pattern that, if stabilized and energized, can condense into the reality you experience.

But thought alone is not enough.

A vague thought is like a faint sketch, easily erased by the stronger patterns of collective consciousness or your own conflicting desires. A clear thought, held steadily, becomes a precise instruction to the field.

Yet even a clear blueprint needs power to move it toward materialization. That power is emotion.

Emotion is vibrational charge. It gives life to the thought-form, energizing it, broadcasting it into the energetic matrix that surrounds and interpenetrates all things. Every feeling you generate — joy, fear, gratitude, anger — carries a frequency. And that frequency determines what you attract, what you repel, what you stabilize.

The stronger and purer the emotional charge, the stronger the transmission.

The more aligned the emotion is with your desire, the faster the manifestation.

This is why idle wishing yields little.
Why frantic begging often repels.
And why quiet, confident certainty attracts.

Your emotional field is your true command center.

Once thought is energized by emotion, it imprints upon the energetic matrix — the unseen field that holds all potential realities. This field has been called by many names: the Akasha, the Quantum Field, the Morphogenetic Field. It is the staging ground where probabilities are organized, where potential begins its descent toward physical form.

At this stage, the manifestation is not yet visible. But it is real. It is growing, stabilizing, drawing into itself the resources, people, opportunities, and circumstances needed for its emergence.

The condensation from the energetic matrix into physical form requires time — not because the system is slow, but because the density of the physical dimension demands sequential organization. Manifestation must thread itself into the already-moving web of causality, weaving its way through the currents of space, time, and existing events.

This is where many falter.

They mistake the time required for form to appear as evidence of failure. They grow impatient. They doubt. And in doubting, they destabilize the very blueprint they labored to create. The field reads their dominant frequency, not their fleeting hopes.

Understand: the field does not respond to words.
It responds to frequency.

And your belief system acts as a gatekeeper at every stage.

Your beliefs — both conscious and unconscious — determine what is allowed to pass from thought into form. If you believe, deep down, that you are unworthy, that your desires are impossible, that life is a battlefield of scarcity and struggle — then your thought-forms, no matter how vivid or energized, will be blocked.

Belief is permission. Lack of belief is prohibition.

This is why changing your external world begins not with rearranging circumstances, but with transforming your internal architecture.

As you believe, so shall you receive.

Every manifestation is a feedback loop.
- Your thought forms the blueprint.
- Your belief grants or denies permission.
- Your emotion fuels or sabotages.
- Your focus sustains or dissolves.
- The field responds, reflecting your internal state.
- The reflection feeds back, reinforcing your belief and emotion.

Most people live within unconscious loops. They create from fear, lack, and doubt — and so they experience more fear, lack, and doubt. Their external world is not their oppressor; it is their mirror.

To break the loop, you must shift the source signal — the thought, the belief, the emotion.

You are not at the mercy of chance.

You are living inside the echo of your own broadcast.

Whether you realize it or not, you are always creating.
- Every thought is a seed.
- Every emotion is a magnet.
- Every belief is a filter.
- Every word is a brushstroke upon the canvas of reality.

The question is not whether you are manifesting, but whether you are doing so consciously or unconsciously.

The field is neutral. It does not judge. It reflects.

It mirrors back to you the sum total of your vibrational state.

This is why superficial affirmations often fail. If you declare, "I am abundant," but internally believe you are trapped in lack, the field responds to the deeper vibration, not the surface words. It is not your mouth that creates; it is your being.

The great Hermetic axiom says it plainly:

"As within, so without. As above, so below."

You cannot fake alignment.
You must become alignment.

Mastery of manifestation is not a trick to get what you want.

It is a path to becoming who you truly are.

When thought, belief, emotion, and focus align — when you operate from the steady, coherent signal of your higher self — the external world reshapes itself around you with breathtaking precision.

Manifestation is not magic.
It is mechanical.

It is the science of mind interacting with the field of potential.

You have always been creating, whether you knew it or not.

The invitation now is to create consciously.

In the chapters that follow, we will explore the specific laws that govern this process — the timeless, unbreakable principles by which thought becomes form, by which intention becomes reality.

**The system is waiting.
The field is listening.
Your future is already forming.**

Now, you will learn how to command it — not by force, but by alignment.

Belief and the Permission Matrix

Now that you have glimpsed the true architecture of reality creation — how thought forms arise, how emotion fuels, how the energetic field responds — we arrive at one of the most subtle, most misunderstood, and most crucial elements of manifestation: belief.

It is not your desire that determines what you experience.
It is not your willpower.
It is not even the vividness of your visualization.

It is your belief — the unseen gatekeeper that quietly decides whether your thought-form is permitted to pass into the field of creation or whether it will collapse back into potential, unrealized.

Belief is not a concept. It is not simply an idea you hold in your mind.

It is a program — a deep structure embedded within your personal operating system.

It governs what your reality field allows.

You may desire great abundance, vibrant health, profound love. You may visualize these outcomes with passion. But if your core beliefs — most of which reside beneath your conscious awareness — declare that these things are not available to you, not safe for you, not possible for you, the system will quietly reject your commands.

Belief is permission.
Lack of belief is prohibition.

This system is not cruel.
It is precise.

The God Mind operates according to laws that honor your free will at the deepest levels. Your beliefs are treated as your chosen instructions. They are not imposed upon you; they are accepted by you — even if you accepted them unconsciously, even if they were planted by others long ago.

This entire structure — this lattice of invisible permissions — is what I call your Permission Matrix.

The Permission Matrix is the sum total of what you allow yourself to experience as real. It defines the boundaries of your world. It holds the rules you have internalized about what is possible for you.

And here lies one of the great paradoxes of manifestation:

You do not manifest what you want.
You manifest what you believe.

Two people may desire the same thing. One achieves it effortlessly; the other struggles endlessly. The difference lies not in luck, not in virtue, not in hard work, but in the permissions embedded within their respective matrices.

The most dangerous beliefs are not the ones you know you hold.

They are the silent ones you have never questioned.

From childhood, you have been programmed.

Your parents spoke their fears into your listening mind:
"Money doesn't grow on trees."
"You have to struggle to succeed."
"People like us don't get ahead."

Your culture handed you its limitations:
"Only certain people deserve power."
"Love is hard to find."
"Illness is inevitable."

Your religion may have delivered its warnings:
"Desire is sinful."
"Wealth is corrupting."
"Suffering earns virtue."

Your society whispered its consensus:
"Life is hard."
"Success is rare."
"You are limited."

Each of these became threads in your Permission Matrix — often woven so early, so deeply, that you accepted them as reality itself.

But these are not universal truths. They are local agreements — arbitrary thought-forms stabilized by repetition and collective reinforcement. They are not absolute laws of existence; they are inherited programs.

The Permission Matrix holds them in place until you consciously revoke them.

And this is the crux of true manifestation:

Your desire must pass through this Matrix to enter the field.

If your Matrix rejects it, it does not matter how much you want it, how vividly you visualize it, or how sincerely you hope for it. The system will default to your dominant belief.

This is why so many spiritual seekers, so many earnest manifestors, feel frustrated. They affirm, they meditate, they declare — but they do so while carrying silent permissions that block their very desire.

They say:
"I am abundant."
But their Matrix whispers:

"I will never escape debt."
They declare:
"I am loved."
But their Matrix hums:
"I am not worthy."

**The field does not respond to your mouth.
It responds to your Matrix.**

This is not a flaw in the system. It is its perfection.

The God Mind, in its infinite wisdom, honors your deepest permissions as your sovereign choice — even when those permissions work against you.

The field always answers: "As you believe, so shall you receive."

Understand this: belief is not mere opinion.

Opinions are surface thoughts. They change easily.

Beliefs are structural frameworks. They define your very perception of reality.

Two people can witness the same event — one sees opportunity, the other sees threat — because their Permission Matrices interpret the event through entirely different codes.

This system becomes self-reinforcing.

**You believe money is scarce.
You fail to attract abundance.
The lack reinforces your belief.
The cycle deepens.**

Most humans live trapped within these closed loops, generating reality fields that simply replay the permissions they have not yet reprogrammed.

But here lies your liberation:

Belief is programmable.

Your Matrix is not fixed. It is not an immutable law. It is a flexible structure that can be rewritten.

You were programmed — but you can reprogram.

This is the real spiritual initiation: the conscious, methodical rewriting of your Permission Matrix. You are not waiting for life to change. You are changing the very system through which life responds.

The process is clear:
1. Identify your limiting beliefs.
2. Observe their origins without blame or guilt.
3. Challenge their validity through higher truth.
4. Replace them with beliefs that reflect your soul's true nature.
5. Install the new permissions through repetition and emotional reinforcement.

The more you expand your Permission Matrix, the more freely your desires flow into the field. At advanced levels of mastery, your permissions become vast:
- You believe health is your default state.
- You believe abundance flows naturally.
- You believe love is abundant and safe.
- You believe creation is your rightful act.

And as you believe, so your world reflects.

At the highest truth, your Permission Matrix is the interface between your Fractal Mind and the Infinite Field. It is how free will is honored. The God Mind does not impose reality upon you — It mirrors back your deepest instructions.

This is not punishment. It is cosmic respect.
The field says only:

"I will give you what you allow yourself to receive."

You are the author.
The code responds.

In the chapters ahead, we will now explore how this Permission Matrix interfaces with your emotional energy, your vibrational frequency, and your full manifestation system.

The game is not rigged against you.
You simply inherited old rules.
And now you are ready to rewrite them.
You were never denied your power.
You were only trained to forget it.

Now you will remember.

Emotional Energy and Vibrational Law

You have now seen the architecture. You understand that thought is the blueprint, belief is the permission, and the field responds to the totality of your internal state. But there is one force within this system that acts as the engine — the power source that determines whether your manifestation flickers weakly or roars into being with unstoppable force.

That engine is emotion.

Most have misunderstood emotion. They see it as a byproduct of experience, as something that happens after life unfolds. Joy comes when circumstances turn favorable; fear arrives when danger appears; anger rises when offense is given. In this view, emotion is reactive — a slave to the external.

But for the practitioner of manifestation, emotion is not a response.

Emotion is cause.
Emotion is not secondary. It is primary.

It is the frequency you broadcast into the energetic field. It is the signal the Universe reads and reflects.

If thought is the design, and belief is the gate, then emotion is the current that carries the signal across the dimensions.

The ancient sages understood what modern quantum science is only beginning to confirm: beneath the illusion of solidity, everything vibrates. Every atom, every molecule, every cell, every structure — all are oscillating fields of energy.

Nothing is truly still. Reality itself is vibration stabilized into form.

You, too, are vibration. Your consciousness emits frequency at every moment — and your emotional state determines that frequency.

Joy vibrates differently than sorrow.
Gratitude emits a different resonance than fear.
Certainty hums at a higher frequency than doubt.

The field is responsive to these frequencies.

It arranges your reality to match your dominant emotional broadcast.

You are like a transmitter, broadcasting signals into the energetic matrix that surrounds and interpenetrates all things. The field does not analyze your words. It does not interpret your affirmations at the surface level. It mirrors back the vibration you emit.

This is the great secret of manifestation that so many miss:

You do not attract what you think you want.
You attract what you emotionally radiate.

Two people may hold the same desire. One succeeds effortlessly, the other struggles endlessly. The difference lies not in their words or mental clarity alone, but in the frequency of emotion they bring to the desire.

Emotion is not mere feeling.
It is vibrational power.

Consider the vibrational spectrum of emotion as a ladder, each step a higher or lower frequency:

- Very High: Love, bliss, ecstasy, unconditional gratitude.

- High: Joy, peace, certainty, confidence.
- Medium: Contentment, acceptance, mild hope.
- Low: Anxiety, worry, frustration, doubt.
- Very Low: Fear, shame, guilt, despair.

As you ascend this ladder, your signal grows more coherent, more powerful, more attractive to the realities that match your desire. As you descend, your signal grows chaotic, fragmented, and magnetizes struggle, delay, and distortion.

This is not punishment. It is not moral judgment.

It is simply the mechanical response of a vibrational system.

The Universe mirrors your state.

If you carry fear while affirming abundance, you attract more experiences that justify your fear. If you cultivate gratitude even before the manifestation arrives, you accelerate its arrival. Emotion leads the frequency. Frequency shapes reality.

But here is where many falter: they attempt to force positivity.

They repeat hollow affirmations.
They paste smiles over anxiety.
They pretend gratitude while feeling desperate.

The field reads not your pretense, but your core frequency.

Forced positivity is incoherent.
Authentic emotional alignment is coherent.

The goal is not to suppress lower emotions or deny

their presence. Suppression creates conflict; conflict creates resistance; resistance blocks manifestation. The path is to heal, to clear, to release — so that authentic high-frequency states emerge naturally.

You do not manufacture joy.
You restore it by clearing what obscures it.

Of all emotional frequencies, one stands as supreme in the manifestation process: certainty.

Certainty is not arrogance.
It is not bravado.

It is the calm, steady knowing that your manifestation already exists in the field — even if your senses have not yet perceived its arrival.

Hope says, "I wish this could happen."
Certainty says, "It is done."

The field responds to certainty with unmatched precision.
Certainty stabilizes your signal, eliminating doubt, quieting conflict, allowing the dimensional processing of your manifestation to proceed without interruption.
Paired with certainty is another master frequency: gratitude.
Gratitude, especially when practiced in advance of receiving, acts as a magnetic amplifier. It assumes receipt. It broadcasts to the field, "I have already received what I desired." In doing so, it collapses the timeline between desire and fulfillment.
When you feel genuine gratitude for your future manifestation as if it is already present, you are encoding the field with a completed vibrational blueprint.

Gratitude is the emotional signature of receipt.

The system rewards those who master emotional coherence — when thought, belief, and emotion are fully aligned. In this state, the field receives a clean, undistorted transmission. Manifestation becomes not a battle, but an unfolding.

Incoherence, on the other hand, creates static.

You may visualize wealth, but if you carry guilt about receiving it, the static cancels your signal. You may desire love, but if you fear vulnerability, the field receives contradiction. Mixed signals slow or collapse the manifestation process entirely.

Emotional mastery is vibrational mastery.
Vibrational mastery is manifestation mastery.

Your emotional state is not something that happens to you.
It is something you cultivate.

You are not a victim of emotional weather.
You are the climate itself.

When you fully grasp this, you begin to take responsibility for your emotional broadcast at every moment. You stop waiting for circumstances to dictate how you feel, and instead use your inner state to reshape your circumstances.

This is the reversal of unconscious living:
No longer does reality shape your emotions.
Now, your emotions shape your reality.

The system responds to who you are being — not who you wish to be.

> You do not attract what you seek.
> You attract what you embody.
> You are always transmitting.
> You are always receiving.
> You are always creating.

In the next chapter, we will move deeper into the laws that govern this entire system. We will step beyond these foundational principles into the Eight Laws of Manifestation — the complete operating blueprint that governs every act of creation within the field.

> Master the laws, and you master the game.
> You have always been broadcasting.

> Now, you will broadcast by design.

The Eight Laws of Manifestation

Manifestation is not a mystery. It is not a game of chance, nor a matter of luck, nor the capricious favor of unseen forces. Though many have reduced it to superstition, or distorted it into magical thinking, manifestation remains what it has always been — a system. And like any true system, it operates according to laws.

These laws are not arbitrary. They were not invented by gurus, nor whispered by chance. They are woven into the very structure of reality itself. They are the blueprint upon which the Infinite God Mind creates and upon which every Fractal Mind — every soul, every consciousness — participates in creation.

Whether you are aware of them or not, these laws are active.

Whether you believe in them or not, they govern every outcome you experience.

Whether you understand them or not, they shape your world every single moment.

Most humans live within the field of these laws unconsciously. They create by default, driven by beliefs and emotions they have never examined, producing lives that often feel chaotic, unfulfilled, or stuck in cycles they cannot seem to break. But those who awaken — those who come to understand the architecture — begin to participate in these laws deliberately. They become not passive recipients of life, but conscious creators within it.

You have now reached that point.

The curtain is pulled back.
The system will no longer operate in secret.

Here are the Eight Laws of Manifestation — the living framework through which all reality creation unfolds:

LAW 1 — The Law of Mental Primacy

Everything begins in Mind.
Mind is not a byproduct of matter.
Matter is a byproduct of Mind.

The God Mind, the Infinite Source, holds all realities as thought-forms, as emanations of pure consciousness. Every galaxy, every dimension, every molecule, every circumstance arises first within Mind and only then crystallizes into form.

There is no existence outside of Mind. All that is, is thought within the Infinite. The physical world — as solid as it may appear — is merely stabilized mental projection. Your own Fractal Mind operates within this larger field, forming thoughts that, when aligned with belief, emotion, and focus, extend into the same creative system.

Every act of manifestation begins here:

You think. Creation responds.
Without thought, nothing can form.
With thought, manifestation begins.

LAW 2 — The Law of Fractal Participation

You are not separate from the Source.
You are a living extension of the Infinite God Mind.
You carry within you Its architecture, scaled into your individualized consciousness.

You were not cast into existence as a spectator. You were projected into this field as a participant. You have inherited the divine structure that allows thought to become form. You are authorized — by design — to create.

**Creation is not something that happens to you.
It happens through you.**

Every thought you hold, every belief you cultivate, every emotion you fuel — all of these are acts of creation. Whether you know it or not, you are shaping reality at all times. To become a practitioner is not to gain new powers; it is to become conscious of the powers you have always wielded.

LAW 3 — The Law of Belief Dominance

**Belief is the gatekeeper of manifestation.
You do not receive what you merely desire.
You receive what your internal permissions allow.**

Your Permission Matrix — the lattice of conscious and unconscious beliefs you carry — filters every thought you attempt to manifest. If your beliefs permit the manifestation, it proceeds into the field freely. If your beliefs resist it, the signal collapses before it can stabilize.

**Desire without belief is powerless.
Desire with aligned belief is unstoppable.**

This is why so many struggle in their manifestations. They want one thing while believing something entirely different beneath the surface. The system does not respond to words; it responds to the dominant permission held within your Matrix.

As you believe, so shall you receive.

LAW 4 — The Law of Attention and Focus

Energy follows attention.
Where you direct your focus, you direct your creative power.

Your attention stabilizes the blueprint you are broadcasting. A scattered mind sends a fragmented signal. A focused mind concentrates the blueprint into coherence.

If you hold your desire weakly, fleetingly, or with divided attention, the energetic structure dissolves. If you hold it steadily, with clarity and consistency, the field locks onto your signal and begins organizing circumstances accordingly.

Focus is not obsession.
It is not anxious clinging.

It is steady, relaxed, confident alignment with the vision you have chosen.

Where your attention goes, manifestation flows.

LAW 5 — The Law of Emotional Charge

Emotion is the fuel of manifestation.
It powers the thought-form into vibrational motion.

Thought creates the structure.
Belief permits the structure.
Emotion energizes and amplifies the structure.

The vibrational frequency of your emotional state determines:
- What you attract (frequency match).
- How strongly you attract (amplitude).

- How quickly you attract (velocity).

Joy, love, gratitude, certainty — these are high-frequency states that supercharge your manifestation. Fear, doubt, guilt, or desperation inject static into your signal, weakening or distorting the process.

The Universe is vibrational.
Emotion determines your signal strength.

LAW 6 — The Law of Non-Resistance

What you resist, you block.
What you allow, you empower.

Resistance introduces contradiction into your broadcast. Doubt, fear, urgency, and attachment to control all inject interference into the manifestation process.

Manifestation is not forced into being.
It is allowed into being.

The master practitioner does not obsessively attempt to control the "how" or "when" of the unfolding. Instead, they release resistance, trusting the intelligent orchestration of the field.
True non-resistance is not passive laziness.
It is confident surrender.

You hold the vision.
You fuel it with emotion.
You release conflict.

The field handles the unfolding.

LAW 7 — The Law of Divine Alignment

The highest manifestations are those aligned with your soul's evolutionary path and with the greater harmony of the God Mind's unfolding.

When your desires serve not only personal gratification, but also your growth, your contribution, and the upliftment of others, the field accelerates your manifestation.

The God Mind favors evolution.

It supports expansion, service, harmony, and the fulfillment of soul contracts.

Ego-driven desires, rooted in fear or vanity, often produce unstable results or karmic consequences.

Soul-aligned desires flow effortlessly, sustainably, and with extraordinary synchronicity.

When you align with the Infinite, the Infinite aligns with you.

LAW 8 — The Law of Dimensional Processing

Manifestation unfolds across multiple dimensions.
While creation is instant at the level of Mind, physical materialization requires sequencing.

In the higher, non-physical dimensions, thought and reality are one. But in dense physical reality, manifestations must pass through the mechanics of space, time, causality, and complex coordination.

Delays are not denials.

They are the processing time required for your manifestation to integrate harmoniously into the web of existing reality.

Time allows:
- Coordination of people and circumstances.
- Synchronization with other souls' paths.
- Protection from premature or destabilizing arrivals.

The master practitioner understands that patience is not passive waiting, but confident trust in perfect unfolding.

THE INTEGRATED SYSTEM

When these Eight Laws are seen not as isolated principles, but as a single, unified operating system, the full process of manifestation reveals itself with breathtaking simplicity:
- You think (Mental Primacy).
- You are authorized (Fractal Participation).
- You believe (Belief Dominance).
- You focus (Attention).
- You feel (Emotional Charge).
- You release (Non-Resistance).
- You align (Divine Alignment).
- You allow (Dimensional Processing).

The system receives your signal and reflects it back as your lived experience.

You were never waiting for the system to start working.
You were always inside it.
Now, you are learning to operate it consciously.

You have always been manifesting.

The question was never whether you create, but whether you create by accident or by design.

With these laws fully revealed, you stand at the threshold of mastery.

You are no longer guessing at how reality responds.

You are learning how to direct it, as you were always meant to.

In the chapters to come, we will now explore the work of clearing internal resistance, aligning your soul's highest path, and applying these laws in every area of your life.

The system is now visible.
The laws are unchanging.

The practitioner rises.

The Role of the Unconscious and Collective Mind

There is a silent force that moves beneath the surface of every manifestation. It whispers beneath your thoughts, shapes your desires, colors your emotions, and weaves itself into the fabric of your personal reality. It is invisible to the untrained eye, yet it exerts a profound influence on everything you attempt to create.

That force is your unconscious mind — and woven into it is something even larger: the vast field of the Collective Mind.

If you imagine your conscious mind as a small, illuminated island, then your unconscious is the great, unexplored ocean that surrounds it. This ocean is not dead water. It is teeming with programs, inherited beliefs, unhealed wounds, cultural conditioning, and ancestral patterns — most of which you did not choose, and most of which you do not even realize you carry.

The unconscious mind is not your enemy.
It is not a saboteur by nature.

It is a protective system — one that was built, layer by layer, to help you survive, to make sense of your early world, to stabilize your identity amidst complexity.

But what it stabilizes may not serve you.
In fact, it may actively block you.

For as you seek to create new realities — wealth, health, love, purpose — your unconscious mind holds the keys to your Permission Matrix. And if it holds permissions rooted in fear, scarcity, unworthiness, or inherited trauma, your conscious desires will collide with silent barriers you cannot see but will feel.

You will experience the collision as frustration, stagnation, repeated failure, or mysterious reversals of fortune. You will feel as though something resists you. And indeed, something does: your own unexamined programming.

But you are not only swimming in your personal unconscious.

You are also immersed in the vast energetic field of the Collective Mind.

The Collective Mind is not a metaphor.
It is real.

It is the shared field of thought-forms, beliefs, and emotional imprints generated by humanity as a whole across countless generations.

This Collective Field is composed of:
- Generational wounds
- Cultural assumptions
- Religious doctrines
- Scientific paradigms
- Political narratives
- Historical traumas
- Mass fears
- Shared hopes and anxieties

Every family, every tribe, every nation, every civilization contributes to it.

You were born into it. You absorbed it long before you knew you were absorbing.

From your earliest moments, you inherited these collective permissions:

- "Money is scarce."
- "Illness is random and inevitable."
- "Aging equals decline."
- "Power belongs to a select few."
- "War is inevitable."
- "Suffering is noble."
- "You must struggle to survive."

These permissions are not universal truths.

They are long-running programs — stabilized through repetition, cultural agreement, and the sheer gravitational pull of mass consensus.

The longer these beliefs circulate, the more real they seem. The more people who hold them, the stronger they are encoded into the Collective Matrix. Over centuries, they harden into what appears as unchangeable reality.

But here is the great secret:

Consensus is not truth. It is momentum.

Much of what you believe to be "the way life is" is simply the accumulated residue of collective permission fields you have unconsciously consented to inhabit.

The Collective Mind has shaped your unconscious more deeply than you realize:

- Your parents downloaded its programs into you as they repeated their inherited fears.
- Your schools reinforced it as they trained you in "how the world works."
- Your religions codified it as moral law.
- Your media saturated you with it through endless repetition.
- Your culture wrapped it in identity and belonging.

By the time you reached adulthood, you were carrying a

Permission Matrix that was not purely your own creation, but a complex layering of generations of collective programming.

And herein lies one of the greatest challenges in mastering manifestation:

You are not only clearing personal resistance — you are untangling your mind from the gravity of collective agreement.

The question many practitioners ask is sobering:

"If billions believe in limitation, can my small personal belief overcome them?"

The answer is: Yes — but with nuance.

In the private domains of your life — your health, your finances, your relationships, your soul's purpose — your personal Permission Matrix holds supreme authority. The field responds to your broadcast. You can withdraw consent from collective scarcity, disease, or dysfunction and live within an entirely different stream of reality.

But in collective domains — global affairs, politics, mass events — your personal manifestation interacts with the inertia of billions of minds. Change at this scale requires the rising of many individuals shifting their Permission Matrices in parallel, tipping the balance of the collective field.

You do not transform the Collective Mind by force. You transform it by frequency contribution.

Every individual who clears their resistance, who embodies high-frequency creation, who lives as a sovereign practitioner — each one broadcasts stabilizing codes into the Collective Field. And as more awaken, the entire lattice begins to shift.

The Collective Mind is not fixed.

It is evolving.
Humanity is ascending through progressive stages:
- From survival consciousness
- Into scarcity consciousness
- Into victim consciousness
- Into creator consciousness
- Into unity consciousness

As you clear your personal field, you become part of this larger wave. You become both student and architect of planetary evolution. Your personal work is never purely personal. Every healing, every awakening, every manifestation you master becomes a ripple in the great field, subtly but surely weakening the gravity of the old Collective Matrix.

But understand: this requires vigilance.

For even the awakened practitioner remains susceptible to the pull of collective gravity. It whispers in every news headline, every conversation rooted in fear, every mass narrative of doom.

The path of mastery requires that you become sovereign over your mind. You must observe where collective programs attempt to reinstall themselves. You must continually reclaim authorship of your Permission Matrix.

- You are not required to participate in collective poverty.
- You are not required to participate in collective illness.
- You are not required to participate in collective fear.
- You are not required to participate in collective limitation.
- You choose.
- You withdraw consent.
- You recalibrate.

The master practitioner stands inside the world but operates above its gravitational field.

You walk among the collective, but you vibrate from a higher frequency stream.

You become a transmitter of coherence, not a receiver of distortion.

This is not isolation. It is leadership.
You are not escaping the world.

You are uplifting it through your presence, your creations, your example.

With every manifestation you align, you pierce the veil of collective limitation. You carve pathways through the dense web of old agreements, allowing others to follow.

You are not simply manifesting personal outcomes.
You are participating in the healing of the Collective Mind.

This is the sacred responsibility of the practitioner.

In the chapters to come, we will now explore one of the most mysterious and often misunderstood aspects of manifestation: Divine Timing and Dimensional Processing — why your manifestations sometimes seem delayed, and how the field organizes complex creations across multiple layers of existence.

You will learn how to trust the orchestration of the Infinite.

The field is never failing you.
It is always aligning you.

Divine Timing and Dimensional Processing

You have now come to understand the powerful architecture that underlies all creation. You have seen that thought initiates, belief permits, emotion fuels, and the field responds. But as many practitioners encounter, there remains one great point of frustration, one persistent source of doubt, one question that can shake even the most devoted student of manifestation:

"Why hasn't it arrived yet?"

The mind asks:

"If I have done everything correctly—if my thought is clear, my belief is aligned, my emotion is elevated, and my focus is steady—why do I not see the evidence of my creation in my physical reality?"

This moment of apparent delay has caused many to abandon the practice altogether.
Some decide the process does not work.
Some believe they have failed.
Some assume the Universe has denied their request.

But what is most often misunderstood is that this apparent delay is not a failure.

It is not a rejection.
It is not even truly a delay.
It is Dimensional Processing.

To understand this, you must see beyond the limits of linear time. You must begin to think like the field itself — beyond the boundaries of human impatience, beyond the surface illusions of sequence and struggle. You must learn to see creation as it actually unfolds: across dimensions, across layers of reality, governed by intricate timing that serves the highest harmony of the Whole.

At the level of pure Mind — the realm of Source — creation is instantaneous.

The moment you declare a desire from an aligned state, it is already complete in the energetic blueprint. The signal is transmitted. The field has responded. The outcome exists as a stabilized pattern within the higher dimensional framework.

But you do not live solely in the realm of pure Mind.

You are incarnated in the realm of density — the physical plane — where thought must condense into form through multiple layers of energetic scaffolding.

Imagine creation as a multi-layered descent:
- First, your Fractal Mind receives the desire as an inspired thought.
- Second, your belief structure filters the desire, permitting or denying its passage.
- Third, your emotional field activates the energetic frequency of your desire.
- Fourth, the energetic matrix begins to organize potential elements that will form your reality.
- Finally, your manifestation begins to condense into physical form — through people, events, circumstances, opportunities, and interactions.

This process is not instantaneous because physical reality operates within space, time, inertia, and interconnection. Manifestation is not occurring in isolation. It must harmonize with the infinitely complex web of other beings, other intentions, other soul contracts, other manifestations that are unfolding simultaneously.

The field is not simply delivering your desire.
It is orchestrating the perfect unfolding of your desire.

Consider the analogy of planting a seed. You do not bury the seed and expect a towering tree to emerge by morning. The seed germinates beneath the soil. The roots must anchor. The sprout must push upward. The leaves must unfurl. The tree grows in perfect sequence, even when you cannot yet see its progress.

Your manifestation operates the same way.

In these unseen early stages, many falter because they mistake the invisible phase of construction for stagnation. They do not realize the field is already arranging their creation behind the veil.

At the higher levels of reality, your manifestation already exists as pure form.

What you experience as time is simply the dimensional integration of that form into your physical world.

This processing time serves several sacred functions:

- **Harmonization:** It allows your desire to integrate into the collective web of reality without disrupting the evolutionary flow of other beings.
- **Protection:** It shields you from premature manifestations that could destabilize your life if delivered before you are truly ready to hold them.
- **Alignment:** It ensures that all supporting elements—people, opportunities, resources—are positioned

correctly for your manifestation to flourish sustainably.

Impatience is the enemy of this process, not because it angers the field, but because it introduces vibrational static into your signal. Doubt creeps in. Frustration emerges. The coherent signal you once broadcast becomes fragmented.

The field, ever responsive, reflects this fragmentation by slowing, distorting, or even collapsing the materialization you initiated.

The master practitioner understands that waiting is not inactivity.

It is participation in an ongoing orchestration that is far more intelligent, far more intricate, far more beautiful than your conscious mind can grasp.

This is the realm of Divine Timing.

Divine Timing is not random.
It is not punishment.

It is the field delivering your desire at the moment of highest harmony — when receiving it serves not only your personal expansion, but the broader evolutionary arc of all who are connected to your manifestation.

What you experience as a delay may in fact be:

- The ripening of your own capacity to receive and sustain the manifestation.
- The preparation of other individuals who will play a role in your creation.
- The clearing of karmic entanglements that must be resolved first.
- The unfolding of unseen opportunities that will amplify your manifestation beyond what you initially envisioned.

From your limited vantage point, you see only the absence of arrival.

From the field's vantage point, the system is always in motion — organizing your reality in the most optimal sequence.

This is why some manifestations arrive seemingly overnight, while others unfold across months or years. The complexity of your desire determines the processing time required.

- A parking space may manifest instantly.
- A business empire may require years of coordinated dimensional weaving.
- A soulmate connection may involve decades of soul preparation before perfect convergence.

It is not harder for the field to create large manifestations than small ones. The difference lies in the number of interconnected variables involved.

The more intricate your desire, the more sophisticated the orchestration.

But never confuse complexity with impossibility.

The field never tires.
The field never forgets.
The field never fails.

Your role during dimensional processing is clear:
- Maintain emotional coherence.
- Cultivate certainty.
- Release resistance.
- Trust the unfolding.

Do not dig up your seeds in panic to check their growth. Water them with trust.

Tend to your vibration.

Allow the field to do what it does with perfect intelligence.

The wise practitioner observes the early ripples of manifestation as evidence of processing in motion:

- Unexpected meetings.
- Seemingly random coincidences.
- Synchronicities that align with your desire.
- New ideas or opportunities that feel divinely timed.

These are signals.

They are the early winds announcing the approaching arrival of your creation.

Celebrate these signs. They are the language of the field whispering to you,

"It is unfolding. Stay the course."

There is one final truth you must carry forward:

Creation is always instant. Materialization is always sequential.

The system never says no.

It says either, "Yes now," or "Yes — after dimensional alignment."

When you trust this process fully, you move into effortless co-creation.

You no longer grasp or struggle.
You no longer plead or worry.
You simply allow.

The practitioner of mastery holds the vibration steady while the field arranges the symphony.

In the next chapter, we will now step fully into the

practical methodology of creation — the Seven Stages of Manifestation — where you will be trained in the exact step-by-step system by which every manifestation moves from thought to form.

The architecture has been revealed.
Now, you will learn to operate it.

The real mastery begins.

The Seven Stages of Manifestation

You now stand before the operating system fully revealed. You have learned the architecture of reality, the governing laws of the field, the role of your beliefs, emotions, and focus, and the orchestration of Divine Timing itself. You have seen the great mechanisms behind the veil — how thought becomes blueprint, how belief opens the gate, how emotion fuels the signal, how focus stabilizes it, and how the field responds in perfect sequence.

But now comes the most critical phase of your training: The Method of Execution.

It is not enough to understand the architecture conceptually.

It is not enough to agree with the principles intellectually.

Mastery arises in practice — in the disciplined application of these laws, woven into the fabric of your daily life.

Manifestation is not some mystical event you attempt occasionally, hoping the Universe responds.

Manifestation is your natural operating system.

You are always broadcasting. You are always receiving.

The difference between struggle and mastery is whether you are broadcasting by accident or by design.

The Seven Stages of Manifestation form the complete cycle by which any desire — regardless of its size, complexity, or domain — moves from seed to harvest. This is the formula, universal and unchanging. Every master has used it, whether they named it or not. Every failure in manifestation is a breakdown in one or more of these stages. Every success is the result of their alignment.

Let us now walk, step by step, through this sacred process.

Stage 1: Desire — The Thought-Form Creation

All manifestation begins with desire.
Desire is not a weakness. It is not greed.
It is not selfish to want, nor is it shallow to dream.

Desire is the voice of your soul calling you forward.

It is the evolutionary impulse within you — the encoded signal that guides your expansion, your contribution, and your unfolding mastery. Your desires are not random impulses; they are invitations from your higher self to participate in the great unfolding of your purpose.

When desire first arises, it often appears as a whisper — a quiet longing, a persistent idea, a vision that will not leave. Your role at this stage is to listen deeply, to honor the desire rather than dismiss it.

But desire alone is insufficient. The untrained mind allows desires to remain vague, undefined, drifting like clouds. Vague desires produce vague outcomes.

You must refine the desire into a clear, vivid thought-form.
You must see it.
Feel it.
Name it.
Shape it with precision.

The clearer your vision, the more exact your blueprint becomes. The field does not respond to ambiguity. It responds to specificity.

A blurred blueprint creates a scattered signal.
A sharp blueprint commands the field with certainty.

Stage 2: Intention — The Directive Will

Desire is the recognition of possibility.
Intention is the command.

It is not enough to want. You must choose.

Intention is the moment when your Fractal Mind declares to the field:
"I claim this. I am ready to co-create this reality."

It is the issuing of directive will — not from desperation, not from entitlement, but from calm authority.
Intention stabilizes your desire.
It sends a clear instruction into the fabric of Mind.
It focuses your internal systems, aligning subconscious mechanisms, attention, and emotional alignment toward the outcome.
True intention carries an energetic weight. It is not frantic or needy. It is quiet confidence.

Intention whispers to the field:
"It is done."

Stage 3: Belief Calibration — Permission Activation

Here you confront the first critical gate of manifestation:
Your Permission Matrix.

Your conscious desire may be strong. Your intention may be clear. But if your beliefs contain contradictions, the system will halt.

At this stage, you must examine your inner field with honesty:

- Do you believe this manifestation is truly possible for you?
- Do you feel worthy of its arrival?
- Do you carry silent fears, doubts, or conflicts beneath the surface?

This is where hidden resistance often lurks — inherited beliefs, cultural programming, ancestral wounds, or past failures that whisper,

"This is not allowed."

Your task here is to surface these unconscious blocks, to bring them into awareness without judgment, and to clear them with precision. You may use belief reprogramming techniques, self-inquiry, forgiveness, and conscious affirmation.

Only when your Permission Matrix fully accepts your manifestation does the field receive the green light to proceed without conflict.

Desire without permission is a short circuit.
Desire with permission is a live wire of creative power.

Stage 4: Emotional Resonance — Frequency Activation

Thought is the blueprint.
Belief opens the gate.
Now comes the ignition: emotion.

Emotion is the vibrational charge that sends your signal into the energetic matrix. Without emotional fuel, even the clearest thought-form remains inert. With emotional charge, your blueprint becomes an active magnetic force within the field.

But not all emotions carry the same frequency.
The field responds most powerfully to:

- Joy
- Gratitude
- Love
- Certainty
- Peace

The master practitioner learns to feel the emotional reality of the desire as if it has already arrived. You practice the emotional state of the fulfilled desire in advance, broadcasting the signal of completion before physical evidence appears.

This is the secret of the great masters:

They live emotionally inside their creation before it is visible.

Gratitude, in particular, acts as a powerful amplifier. When you feel genuine gratitude for your manifestation before its arrival, you imprint the field with the frequency of fulfillment.

The field does not wait for proof.
It mirrors your internal state.

Stage 5: Sustained Focus — Attention Stabilization

The field responds not to fleeting wishes but to consistent, stabilized signals.

Here lies one of the great tests of manifestation:

Can you hold your vision steady?

Can you maintain alignment when no physical evidence has yet appeared?

Your focus must become like a steady beam — unwavering, yet relaxed. Obsession weakens the field through anxiety. Indifference scatters the signal. But calm, deliberate focus stabilizes your broadcast.

You engage in daily visualization, emotional rehearsal, and mental alignment. You nourish your desire like a gardener tending the seed — not anxiously digging to check its growth, but steadily watering with confidence.

The longer you sustain focus without collapse, the more coherent and magnetic your signal becomes.

Focus is the stabilizing current.
Wavering focus is the destabilizing static.

Stage 6: Non-Resistance — Surrender of Conflict

At this stage, the practitioner confronts the temptation to control.

You have planted the seed. You have fueled the signal. Now, you must allow.

Non-resistance is the art of releasing attachment to:
- How the manifestation will arrive.
- When it will arrive.
- Through whom or what channel it will arrive.

The field operates with intelligence far beyond your conscious mind. It sees the intricate web of interconnected lives, opportunities, and sequences required for perfect orchestration.

Your job is not to dictate the path.
Your job is to trust the process.

Non-resistance is not passivity.

It is active surrender — the confident knowing that the field is working invisibly, even when your senses see nothing.

Resistance, in the form of impatience, doubt, or micromanagement, injects static into your signal, often slowing or distorting the manifestation.

The master holds the field open and steady:
"I trust. I allow. I receive."

Stage 7: Observation and Reception — Physical Integration

As dimensional processing completes, your manifestation begins to arrive into physical form. Often it will appear not all at once, but through ripples of synchronicity:

- Unexpected meetings
- Sudden opportunities
- Inspired ideas
- Chance conversations
- Subtle signs confirming alignment

These are not coincidences.

They are dimensional echoes, announcing that your creation is materializing.

At this stage, your role is twofold:

- Remain open and observant.
- Take inspired action when opportunities emerge.

Many fail here by dismissing small openings, waiting for some grand arrival. But the field often delivers through natural, organic channels. What seems like coincidence is often the precise door opening into your manifestation.

You must walk through those doors.

When full manifestation arrives, you receive it with gratitude, integrate it into your life, and acknowledge your role in its creation.

This anchors your mastery deeper, reinforcing your field for future manifestations.

The Complete Cycle

To summarize, the Seven Stages of Manifestation are:
1. Desire — Clarify the thought-form.
2. Intention — Issue the directive will.
3. Belief Calibration — Align the Permission Matrix.
4. Emotional Resonance — Charge the frequency.
5. Sustained Focus — Stabilize the signal.
6. Non-Resistance — Allow dimensional orchestration.
7. Observation and Reception — Integrate physical arrival.

This is the Manifestation Operating System.

It is not theory.
It is law.
It is mechanical.
It is universal.

Mastery Is Trained, Not Gifted
No one is born a master.

Manifestation is not a mystical gift reserved for the few.
It is a skill — and like any skill, it is honed through practice, observation, adjustment, and consistency.
Each time you run the cycle, you refine your alignment.
Each success strengthens your confidence.
Each resistance you clear makes the system flow more effortlessly.

You are not becoming a creator.
You have always been a creator.
You are now learning to create with precision.

In the chapters that follow, we will go even deeper — into

the art of breaking internal resistance, aligning your desires with your soul path, and applying this mastery to every area of your life.

The system is installed.
The practice begins.

Breaking Internal Resistance

There is a paradox at the heart of manifestation. On one hand, the system itself is elegantly simple: thought forms reality. And yet, for most, the experience of conscious creation feels endlessly complex, inconsistent, even frustrating. Why?

The answer is resistance.

Resistance is not a failure of willpower, nor a flaw in the laws of manifestation. It is not a moral failing or evidence of personal weakness. Rather, resistance is the natural consequence of two forces meeting: your conscious desire, and your unconscious programming. Where these forces are aligned, manifestation flows easily. Where they are in conflict, manifestation is stalled, distorted, or blocked entirely.

Resistance is not external. It is always internal.

You may consciously declare your desire:
"I choose to manifest abundance."

But beneath that declaration may live ancient, hidden voices whispering:
"I don't deserve it."
"Money is dangerous."
"Success will isolate me."
"Abundance requires sacrifice I cannot bear."

These contradictions are not always immediately visible. They live below the surface of conscious awareness, embedded deep within your Permission Matrix, coded by years — often lifetimes — of inherited beliefs, traumas, cultural conditioning, and unresolved emotional wounds.

To master manifestation is to master the art of purification — the systematic, courageous dismantling of internal resistance.

The clearer your field, the faster your manifestations.

In this chapter, we will move beyond philosophy into precise practice. This is not theoretical. This is the real work.

What Is Resistance?

Resistance is any internal program that silently emits a "no" signal to your conscious "yes."

It may express itself in many forms:

- Limiting beliefs: deeply held conclusions about what is possible, deserved, or safe.
- Emotional wounds: unhealed grief, shame, guilt, or fear connected to past experiences.
- Identity conflicts: subconscious attachments to who you believe you are (or are not).
- Karmic residues: unresolved patterns carried across lifetimes.
- Protective mechanisms: unconscious parts of you attempting to keep you safe by preventing perceived danger.

In essence:
Resistance equals energetic contradiction.

The field always mirrors your dominant energetic signal. If your conscious mind broadcasts "I desire this," but your unconscious broadcasts "this is unsafe," the field receives conflicting instructions. Manifestation is destabilized, delayed, or collapses altogether.

The Energetic Cost of Resistance

Unresolved resistance produces:
- Inconsistent manifestations.
- Repeating cycles of self-sabotage.
- Partial successes followed by sudden collapses.
- Chronic emotional turmoil.
- Exhaustion from effort without result.
- The painful illusion of being "blocked" by fate.

The truth is simpler:
The system works perfectly — even when you feel stuck.
It is faithfully responding to both your desire and your resistance simultaneously.
Mastery arises not from trying harder, but from clearing the contradictions.

The Resistance Purification Framework

We will now enter the core framework of resistance purification. This process is mechanical, repeatable, and lifelong. Every great practitioner revisits it regularly as higher-level desires surface deeper layers of resistance.

The framework consists of five essential stages:
1. Identification — Bring the resistance into conscious awareness.
2. Extraction — Name and externalize the hidden program.
3. Neutralization — Dissolve its emotional charge and logical hold.
4. Reprogramming — Install the aligned belief structure.
5. Stabilization — Reinforce the new permission through repetition and practice.

Let us examine each stage in its full depth.

Stage 1 — Identification: Bringing Resistance Into Awareness

You cannot clear what you cannot see.

The first work is observation. You must become a silent, patient investigator of your own mind.

- Track your self-talk: What stories repeat in your internal dialogue?
- Observe emotional triggers: When do you feel fear, anger, jealousy, guilt, or shame?
- Examine recurring patterns: Where do you repeatedly struggle despite your efforts?
- Reflect on your family history: What financial, relational, or health patterns seem "normal" in your lineage?
- Uncover your worst-case scenarios: What hidden fears live beneath your desires?
- You may ask yourself:
- "If this manifestation fully arrived, what might feel threatening?"
- "What consequences am I subconsciously afraid of?"

Often, resistance is not rooted in doubt about possibility, but fear about what the manifestation would demand.

For example:

- You desire wealth, but fear it will distance you from loved ones.
- You desire a soulmate, but fear intimacy will reopen old wounds.
- You desire success, but fear public exposure will invite criticism.

These unconscious calculations form the roots of resistance.

Rule of Mastery:

Every blocked manifestation contains a hidden protective belief.

Stage 2 — Extraction: Externalizing the Program

Once identified, resistance must be pulled into the light of consciousness.

- Speak it aloud.
- Write it down clearly and specifically.

Example:

"I fear that if I become wealthy, my friends will resent me, and I'll lose connection with them."

This externalization immediately weakens the program's unconscious hold.

By naming it, you transform it from an invisible saboteur into an object of conscious examination.

The principle here is simple:

What you name, you claim authority over.

Stage 3 — Neutralization: Dissolving the Charge

Now you address both the logical and emotional power of the program.

A) Cognitive Deconstruction

- Question its validity:
  "Is this belief objectively true? Always? For everyone?"
- Trace its origin:
  "Where did I first learn this? Was it modeled by parents, culture, religion?"
- Evaluate its usefulness:
  "Does this belief serve my growth, or limit me?"

Most limiting beliefs collapse under the weight of honest logic.

Example:

"Do all wealthy people lose friendships? No. In fact, some attract deeper communities aligned with their values."

B) Emotional Transmutation

- Permit suppressed emotions to surface fully.
- Feel them without resistance.
- Allow grief, fear, anger, or sadness to move through you.

Energy that is fully felt loses its charge.

As the old emotional residue clears, the unconscious link between the desire and the threat dissolves.

C) Compassion and Forgiveness

- Forgive the people or institutions that installed the limiting belief.
- Forgive yourself for carrying it unconsciously.

Forgiveness is not an absolution of harm. It is an energetic release of bondage.

Stage 4 — Reprogramming: Installing the Aligned Belief

Now you install the belief that supports your manifestation.

- Craft the new statement with care:
  "Wealth deepens my ability to serve, connect, and love fully. My success invites aligned, supportive relationships."
- Write it. Speak it. Repeat it.

But repetition alone is not enough.

You must feel the truth of this new belief emotionally. You must charge it with gratitude, certainty, and joy as though it is already active.

- Visualize yourself thriving with this belief in full

operation.
- Experience the emotional relief and expansion that this new permission creates.

The emotional imprinting seals the reprogramming into your field.

Stage 5 — Stabilization: Reinforcing the Permission Matrix

The new belief must be stabilized through repetition until it becomes your automatic operating system.
- Daily affirmations spoken aloud with conviction.
- Regular visualization sessions.
- Emotional rehearsal of the fulfilled state.
- Conscious redirection whenever the old belief attempts to resurface.

Neural pathways rewire through consistency.

The more you engage, the faster the new belief becomes dominant.

Research shows:

A minimum of 21-66 days of consistent reinforcement creates lasting neural reprogramming.

The Cyclical Nature of Resistance Work

Understand: purification is not a one-time event.

Each new level of manifestation exposes deeper layers of resistance. As your desires expand, so will your purification work.
- The resistance you face manifesting $10,000 is different from the resistance of building a global empire.

- The resistance of healing a simple ailment is different from reversing decades of chronic illness.
- The resistance of attracting a relationship is different from sustaining deep, soul-aligned partnership.

This is not failure.
This is evolutionary refinement.

Advanced Forms of Resistance
As you deepen mastery, you will encounter more subtle layers of resistance:

- The Inner Critic: "You're not good enough yet."
- The Victim: "Things never work out for me."
- The Martyr: "I must sacrifice to prove my worth."
- The Guardian: "Change is dangerous; safety lies in the familiar."

Each of these sub-personalities carries protective logic developed from earlier pain. They are not enemies. They are misguided allies.

The master practitioner does not battle these archetypes.

You meet them with compassion, listen to their message, and update their programming with new instructions rooted in safety and growth.

Purification Is Freedom
When resistance is cleared:

- Your desire feels clean and unburdened.
- Emotional coherence becomes natural.
- The signal to the field transmits without distortion.
- Manifestation accelerates with breathtaking ease.

Purification is the foundation of effortless creation.
Clarity creates velocity.

In the next chapter, we will go even deeper — beyond resistance removal — into the sacred art of Alignment with Soul Path and Divine Will.

For manifestation is not merely about obtaining what you want.

It is about becoming who you were designed to be.

The practitioner now enters the highest corridors of mastery — where manifestation becomes not just personal power, but sacred participation in the unfolding intelligence of the Infinite.

Alignment with Soul Path and Divine Will

There is a subtle danger that lurks even for the practitioner who has mastered the architecture of manifestation. It is the temptation to view this power as an instrument for acquiring whatever the ego demands — as though manifestation were a spiritual vending machine, responding to every whim simply because one has learned to press the proper buttons.

This temptation is not new.

It has appeared in every esoteric school, every sacred tradition, every mystery teaching since humanity first glimpsed its latent creative authority. And yet, every true master — every fully awakened practitioner of the God Mind Principle — has eventually discovered the same profound truth:

**The highest manifestation is not about control.
It is about alignment.**

It is not enough to master how reality is formed.
You must also master what you choose to form — and why.
For beneath your conscious desires lies a greater intelligence:
Your Soul Path.

And beyond even your Soul Path, woven into the architecture of the God Mind itself, flows the grand evolutionary impulse of Divine Will.

When your desires serve only personal acquisition, the system responds—but the results are often temporary, unstable, or karmically costly. When your desires are aligned with your Soul Path and Divine Will, the system flows with a kind of effortless grace that can only be described as miraculous.

This is not because the Universe rewards or punishes.

It is because the field itself is self-organizing. It favors coherence.

The Soul Path: Your Individual Blueprint of Evolution

Long before you incarnated into this lifetime, your Fractal Mind — the spark of God Mind that you are — entered into an agreement. A contract was made. Not with some external authority, but with yourself.

You selected:
- The lessons you would seek to master.
- The wounds you would seek to heal.
- The gifts you would seek to activate.
- The forms of service you would offer.
- The stages of growth your soul would navigate.

This is your Soul Path — the unique evolutionary blueprint encoded into your being. It does not dictate every detail of your life, but it establishes the underlying themes, challenges, and opportunities that will arise as you move through your incarnational journey.

The purpose of manifestation is not to avoid this path, but to fully engage it.

**Your desires are signals of your Soul Path —
or distortions of your ego.
Discernment is everything.**

The Two Origins of Desire

Not every desire that arises within you originates from the same source. They emerge from one of two places:

Source	Nature of Desire
Egoic Desire	Rooted in fear, lack, comparison, validation-seeking, avoidance of pain.
Soul-Aligned Desire	Rooted in joy, growth, contribution, self-expression, expansion of consciousness.

Both may feel urgent.
Both may feel convincing.
But their outcomes diverge sharply.

Egoic desires often lead to:
- Temporary satisfaction, followed by restlessness.
- New problems that drain energy.
- Unintended consequences that trigger karmic loops.
- Growing disconnection from inner peace.

Soul-aligned desires lead to:
- Lasting fulfillment.
- Deep internal peace.
- Expanded contribution.
- Accelerated personal evolution.
- Synchronistic, almost magical unfolding.

The Discernment Process: Testing Your Desire

The master practitioner does not automatically pursue every desire.
Instead, you submit each desire to careful inquiry:
- Does this serve my evolutionary growth?

- Does this contribute to the elevation of others?
- Will its fulfillment bring peace or anxiety?
- Does it align with my natural gifts and purpose?
- Would I desire this even if no one else saw or praised me?
- Does this feel like expansion or avoidance?

When a desire survives this examination, it is usually clean.
It carries the unmistakable resonance of the soul.
It feels deep rather than frantic.
It arrives as a knowing rather than a craving.
It calls you forward like the pull of destiny.

The Hidden Cost of Egoic Manifestation

It is true that you can manifest from the ego.
The system does not prevent this, because it honors your free will.

But ego-driven manifestations often create burdens:
- They consume enormous energetic effort.
- They generate side effects that destabilize other life domains.
- They feed the illusion of separation.
- They create karmic entanglements requiring eventual rebalancing.
- They increase anxiety, control patterns, and emotional volatility.

The practitioner who continues creating from the ego finds that each new manifestation demands more control, more effort, more maintenance — until eventually, the weight becomes unsustainable.

Misaligned manifestation always corrects itself over time —often through breakdown, loss, or spiritual exhaustion.

This is not punishment.
It is course correction.

The Ease of Aligned Manifestation

When your desires align with your Soul Path:
- Doors open without forced effort.
- The right people arrive at the right time.
- Opportunities seem to materialize "out of nowhere."
- Inner peace remains steady even before the manifestation fully arrives.
- The field organizes the orchestration in ways you could never plan.

This is not because aligned manifestation is "easier" mechanically.

It is because alignment eliminates contradiction.

You are broadcasting a pure, coherent signal that the field can organize without conflict.

You become like a clear channel through which the God Mind expresses itself without distortion.

Divine Will: The Evolutionary Arc of God Mind

Beyond your individual Soul Path flows something even greater — the infinite evolutionary unfolding of the God Mind itself.

The God Mind is not static.

Though perfect in essence, it seeks ever-expanding expressions of:
- Beauty
- Wisdom

- Complexity
- Love
- Self-awareness

Your Soul Path is a micro-thread woven into this vast cosmic evolution.

When your manifestations serve not only your personal growth but contribute to the expansion of the Whole, you enter the highest corridors of manifestation power. This is where your creations are carried by the full current of universal intelligence.

The God Mind supports what serves its own evolution.

When you manifest in service to that unfolding, you are no longer "pulling" reality toward you —

you are allowing reality to pour through you as an instrument of the Infinite.

Manifestation as Sacred Service

At the highest level, manifestation becomes sacred partnership:

- How does this serve not only my expansion but also the elevation of others?
- How does this creation uplift the Collective Mind?
- How does this contribute to the healing, growth, and awakening of all?

This is not sacrifice.
It is not self-denial.

In truth, aligned service produces the greatest personal fulfillment because it flows through the natural harmonic of your soul design.

What serves the Whole serves you.

What serves you serves the Whole.

This is the highest alignment of manifestation.

The Master Frequency of Trust

Aligned manifestation carries a unique emotional signature:
- Peaceful Certainty.
- No urgency.
- No anxiety.
- No desperation.
- No controlling timelines.
- No obsessing over outcomes.

You walk in deep trust, knowing that what serves your soul will always be delivered in perfect sequence — and that anything withheld is ultimately protective, not punitive.

You release the childish demand of the ego that screams:

"I must have this now!"

And you step into the mature trust of the God Mind Practitioner who whispers:

"It will come when I am ready to hold it fully. Until then, I am whole."

You Are the Instrument

You are not separate from the God Mind.
You are its living fractal.
You are its unique instrument.

- Your highest desires are notes in the eternal symphony.

- Your creations are melodies that contribute to the great harmonic.
- Your evolution is part of the infinite learning of God experiencing Itself.

The more purely you tune yourself to the Infinite, the more powerful and beautiful your manifestations become.

At the highest levels, you no longer chase.
You no longer strain.
You no longer grasp.

You simply become the field.
And the field organizes reality around your state of being.

The Litmus Test of Mastery

Before activating any manifestation, ask yourself these five questions:
1. Does this serve my growth and purpose?
2. Is this free of urgency, fear, or scarcity?
3. Will its fulfillment bring me peace rather than more striving?
4. Does it uplift others as well as myself?
5. Am I willing to allow the field to orchestrate its highest form?

When the answer is yes —
the field responds instantly.
Dimensional processing engages.
The orchestration begins.

You Are a Sacred Participant

Manifestation was never about domination of reality.
It was always about participation in its sacred unfolding.

The ego seeks control.
The soul seeks alignment.

You are not here to bend reality into your personal design.
You are here to awaken fully into your co-creative role
as an extension of the Infinite —
The God Mind in motion.

In the final chapters, we will now enter fully applied
mastery — demonstrating how this process operates
practically across every domain of life:

- Wealth
- Health
- Relationships
- Purpose
- Collective impact

You are ready to move from wisdom to execution.
From philosophy to embodiment.
From practice to full participation.

The highest manifestations await.

Real-World Application and Mastery

You now hold in your hands the architecture of creation. The God Mind Principle no longer lives as an abstract philosophy. It stands revealed as the living mechanism that has governed your reality all along — whether you have created consciously or by default.

From this point forward, there can be no return to unconscious creation.
The practitioner is fully awake.

But understanding the structure is only the first half of mastery. True transformation arises when you bring the full architecture into every area of your life, weaving its laws into your finances, your health, your relationships, your purpose, and your role within the evolving Collective Mind.

This chapter will not offer vague encouragements or empty platitudes. It will provide you with the most precise, deeply researched, fully actionable protocols for applied manifestation mastery. The "how" is everything.

In each domain, you will learn:

- The dominant resistance patterns that most people unconsciously carry.
- The purification methods required to neutralize these blocks.
- The specific application of the Seven Stages of Manifestation.
- The advanced nuances for accelerated manifestation within each domain.

Let us now enter applied creation.

Wealth and Abundance Manifestation

The Universal Principle:
Wealth is not the reward for hard labor.

Wealth is the energetic reflection of alignment with value, permission, and contribution.

Money is neither inherently spiritual nor profane. It is energy — a neutral medium that flows to those whose energetic field permits its arrival.

The Core Blockages:
- Scarcity beliefs inherited from family, religion, or culture.
- Guilt around receiving more than others.
- Fear that wealth will corrupt or isolate.
- Deep identity attachments to struggle as a sign of virtue.
- Subconscious association of money with danger or betrayal.

Purification Protocol:
- Identify your inherited money stories.
  Who taught you what wealth means? What patterns run in your lineage?
- Trace limiting beliefs to their roots.
  Was wealth associated with loss, abandonment, or moral compromise?
- Use the Belief Clearing Protocol (Appendix B).
  Reprogram your Permission Matrix to allow wealth as a natural extension of your purpose.
- Replace the identity of the struggling servant with that of the sovereign contributor.

The Wealth Manifestation Application:

1. Desire: Craft a clear, soul-aligned financial vision rooted in service and expansion, not ego.
2. Intention: Declare with calm authority: "I allow financial abundance to flow as a byproduct of my highest contribution."
3. Belief Calibration: Clear resistance by affirming: "My wealth serves not only myself, but the upliftment of others."
4. Emotional Resonance: Practice daily emotional embodiment of wealth — not in greed, but in relief, gratitude, and freedom.
5. Sustained Focus: Visualize financial freedom as a stable, natural state.
6. Non-Resistance: Release attachment to specific income sources. Allow the field to deliver wealth through the most efficient pathways.
7. Reception: Act decisively on inspired opportunities. Trust unusual avenues of income expansion.

Wealth flows most powerfully through aligned contribution.

Health and Physical Healing Manifestation

The Universal Principle:
Your body is the crystallized extension of your consciousness.
Every cell listens to the dominant broadcast of your mind.

The body is not separate from Mind. It is Mind made visible.

The Core Blockages:
- Collective belief in aging as inevitable decline.
- Genetic determinism myths ("it runs in the family").
- Identification with chronic illness as part of identity.
- Unconscious guilt patterns that punish the body.
- Fear-based attachment to diagnoses.

Purification Protocol:
- Audit your inherited health beliefs.
  What did your family, culture, or medical system teach you about disease and aging?
- Revoke participation in collective decline narratives. Affirm: "My body responds to the intelligence of the God Mind within me."
- Perform emotional clearing of past health traumas or identity attachments to illness.

The Health Manifestation Application:
1. Desire: Visualize your body in its optimal, vibrant expression.
2. Intention: Declare - "I allow my cells to restore themselves according to the original God Mind template of perfect health."
3. Belief Calibration: Reprogram your Permission Matrix to accept healing as natural, not exceptional.
4. Emotional Resonance: Feel genuine gratitude for health, even before physical evidence appears.
5. Sustained Focus: Daily visualize healthy, vibrant bodily function at the cellular level.
6. Non-Resistance: Release timelines and desperation for healing. Allow your cellular intelligence to unfold the repair process.
7. Reception: Follow intuitive nudges regarding nutrition, rest, treatment, and lifestyle changes. The field often delivers through both energetic and

physical avenues.

Health is not manufactured; it is remembered.

Relationships and Soul Partnerships Manifestation

The Universal Principle:
You do not attract what you want.
You attract who you are being.

Relationship manifestation is not about searching for completion.
It is about becoming the vibrational match for the partnership you desire.

The Core Blockages:
- Attachment to past wounds (betrayal, abandonment, unworthiness).
- Fear of intimacy reopening old pain.
- Identity attachments to being "unlucky" in love.
- Desperation disguised as desire.
- Control-based lists of rigid partner criteria.
- Purification Protocol:
- Forgive past partners and release victim narratives.
- Clear identity-level wounds around worthiness.
- Release attachment to being completed by another.

The Relationship Manifestation Application:
1. Desire: Clarify the qualities of partnership that serve your soul growth and mutual expansion.
2. Intention: Declare - "I call forth a relationship aligned with my highest vibration, rooted in mutual evolution."
3. Belief Calibration: Reprogram beliefs that relationships equal suffering, loss, or disappointment.

4. Emotional Resonance: Live daily in the emotional state of already experiencing partnership — joy, security, intimacy.
5. Sustained Focus: Visualize the feeling-tone of partnership, not the specific person.
6. Non-Resistance: Release control of where, when, or through whom this partnership arrives.
7. Reception: Follow inspired actions, synchronicities, and chance encounters.

The partner arrives when you have become the match.

Purpose, Career, and Life Work Manifestation
The Universal Principle:

Your highest work is the natural overflow of your joy aligned with the upliftment of others.

When you manifest your true work, you feel energized rather than drained.

The Core Blockages:
- Fear of stepping into visibility.
- Doubt about the value of your gifts.
- Attachment to conventional career safety structures.
- Scarcity-driven compromises ("purpose doesn't pay").
- Fear of failure or ridicule.
- Purification Protocol:
- Reprogram self-worth to match the magnitude of your gift.
- Clear inherited survival programming that limits risk-taking.
- Release societal definitions of success that do not serve your soul.

The Purpose Manifestation Application:

1. Desire: Clarify where your joy intersects with service to others.
2. Intention: Declare - "I activate my highest work and allow my gifts to serve those who are ready to receive."
3. Belief Calibration: Affirm - "The more I serve in alignment, the more abundance and fulfillment flow naturally."
4. Emotional Resonance: Daily embody the emotional state of already living your purpose.
5. Sustained Focus: Visualize yourself actively expressing your highest work with ease, recognition, and flow.
6. Non-Resistance: Release attachment to how your purpose must appear. Allow the form to evolve.
7. Reception: Follow inspired actions, opportunities, and collaborations as the field unfolds new doors.

Purpose requires courage, not certainty. The path appears as you walk it.

Collective and Global Impact Manifestation

The Universal Principle:
As you awaken, your field becomes a stabilizing force that uplifts the evolution of the Collective Mind itself.

Every personal manifestation adds coherence or distortion to the planetary field.

The Core Blockages:
- Feelings of insignificance ("I can't affect global change").
- Cynicism about the state of the world.
- Subconscious participation in collective fear or victim consciousness.

- Resentment toward humanity's perceived failures.
- Purification Protocol:
- Release the illusion of separation from the Collective Mind.
- Accept your role as a stabilizing node in the planetary matrix.
- Clear inherited collective despair and futility programs.

The Collective Manifestation Application:
1. Master personal alignment first.
2. Radiate stability, peace, and unconditional coherence into the field daily.
3. Support others by modeling aligned creation rather than preaching ideology.
4. Contribute solutions, innovations, and compassionate action where your gifts apply.
5. Transmit higher frequencies into the Collective Mind through your state of being.

The global field evolves as enough individuals stabilize higher harmonics.

The Living State of Manifestation Mastery

At full embodiment, manifestation becomes your default operating system:
- You no longer chase or force.
- Desires arise cleanly and naturally.
- Resistance is swiftly identified and dissolved.
- Emotional coherence is a stable state.
- Manifestations arrive in perfect dimensional timing.
- You feel no urgency, no scarcity, no lack.
- You create not for proof, but as sacred participation.

You have become the **God Mind Practitioner** —

not someone who "manifests" occasionally, but one who lives as the field itself.

The more aligned you become, the less effort is required.

You Are the Living Embodiment

At this stage:
- Desires feel like gentle, natural invitations from your higher self.
- Action flows from inspired clarity, not anxious compulsion.
- The field feels like a trusted partner, not an external force.
- Reality itself begins to reorganize around your stable state of being.

You have not bent the system to your will.
You have become one with its operation.

This is true mastery.

In the final section, we will now enter the Closing Transmission — where we seal your full transformation into the role of the God Mind Practitioner.

The full circle is about to complete.

Becoming a God Mind Practitioner

The journey you have undertaken through these pages was never truly about learning something new. At its core, it has been a journey of remembering — the gradual unveiling of a truth that has always lived quietly within you, waiting to be reclaimed.

You have remembered that you are not a prisoner of circumstance.
You are not a servant of external forces.
You are not at the mercy of fate.

You are — and always have been — a Fractal Mind, a living extension of the Infinite God Mind. You are a sovereign co-creator of reality itself.

From the formless depths of the God Mind emerged the architecture you now understand:

- The structure of Mind as First Cause.
- The laws that govern the transmission of thought into form.
- The mechanisms of resistance that interrupt manifestation.
- The purification of belief that unlocks your field.
- The alignment with soul and Infinite Will that transforms power into sacred purpose.
- The mastery of dimensional sequencing that allows you to trust the unfolding.

You are no longer a seeker.
You are now a participant.

The End of Passive Living

Where once you may have approached life as something that happens to you, you now recognize that life is something that unfolds through you.

- Every thought you nurture constructs your reality.
- Every belief you hold frames what you allow to exist.
- Every emotion you cultivate fuels the velocity of creation.
- Every action you take organizes the field to deliver its mirrored expression.

You no longer live reactively.
You live creatively.

You do not beg the Universe for scraps of favor.
You command the field through alignment.

Not through force.
Not through control.
But through the precision of your being.

The Sacred Responsibility of Mastery

The God Mind Principle grants profound power — but it is not power as the world commonly defines it. It is not domination. It is not manipulation. It is not self-indulgence.

It is sacred responsibility.

- To create in harmony with your evolutionary path.
- To uplift yourself without diminishing others.
- To serve the greater unfolding of the God Mind itself.
- To stabilize higher frequencies within the Collective Mind.
- To hold coherent, clean desire free of desperation

or distortion.

- To act as a living transmission of peace, clarity, and expansion.

You create not simply for your own sake, but as a contributor to the great harmonic architecture of existence.

Every pure manifestation uplifts the Whole.
Every alignment you embody sends ripples into the Collective Field.
Every act of creation, when rooted in truth, participates in the evolutionary intelligence of the Infinite.

You are both student and architect in the same breath.

The Field Awaits Your Signal

The God Mind is not distant. It is not passive. It is not silent.

It listens — always — to the transmissions you send into the field.

- Your intentions.
- Your emotional resonance.
- Your belief structures.
- Your degree of resistance or coherence.

There is nothing outside of this interactive matrix.

Every result you experience is the precise echo of your energetic broadcast.

The field never withholds.
It only mirrors.

You have never been denied.
You have only been reflected.

You Are Now the Practitioner

As you stand at the threshold of this work, you do so as a fully equipped God Mind Practitioner — not in theory, but in living practice.

You now embody:
- The full understanding of Mind as the First Cause.
- The mastery of thought-form creation.
- The calibration of belief as permission.
- The precision of emotional resonance as fuel.
- The skill of sustained focus as stabilization.
- The art of non-resistance as surrender.
- The discipline of soul alignment as purification.
- The trust in dimensional timing as orchestration.

You no longer wait for reality.
You broadcast reality.

Mastery Is Embodiment

Though you have learned the system, mastery itself is not knowledge — mastery is embodiment.

Mastery is when:
- You no longer question your role as creator.
- You no longer negotiate your worthiness to receive.
- You no longer fear resistance, but greet it as refinement.
- You no longer seek signs, but live as the signal.
- You no longer struggle to create — you stabilize being, and reality organizes itself accordingly.

At the highest levels of mastery, manifestation becomes so natural that it ceases to feel like effort. You are simply walking as the field itself.

You no longer practice manifestation.
You have become manifestation.

The Evolution Continues

Even as you stand fully equipped, know that the path remains alive.

- The Collective Mind is evolving rapidly.
- The planetary field is accelerating into higher harmonics.
- More Fractal Minds awaken every day.
- Your personal mastery contributes directly to this collective ascension.

You are both a product of the evolution and a participant in accelerating it.

You no longer serve the system.
You now serve its evolution.

The Final Transmission

Remember always:
- You were never powerless.
- You were never separate.
- You were never random.

You have always been:
- A spark of the Infinite God Mind.
- A conscious architect within the eternal field.
- A living instrument of Mind unfolding itself.

This book has not given you power.

It has reawakened your awareness of the power you have always carried.

And now, fully awake, fully equipped, fully aligned —

You create.

Appendices

Appendix A — The Daily Manifestation Practice: Your Daily Alignment Ritual

Mastery is not an event; it is a rhythm.

Manifestation does not arise from occasional inspiration, but from consistent alignment. The God Mind Practitioner understands that each day is both a creative act and a calibration of frequency. Thus, the following daily practice is designed not as a ritual of superstition, but as an energetic hygiene that maintains coherence, dissolves resistance, and sustains the practitioner's manifestation field.

This daily practice becomes your sacred meeting with the God Mind — a place where intention, emotion, and field are continually synchronized.

The Morning Alignment: The Activation of the Day (15–20 minutes)

1 - Centering Breathwork (2 minutes)
The first act of the day is not to react to the world, but to command your internal state. You begin with conscious breath:
- Inhale slowly to a count of four.
- Hold for a count of four.
- Exhale smoothly for a count of four.
- Repeat, establishing stillness.

The breath is your anchor into the field of the present. With this, you arrive fully in the Now — the only space where manifestation operates.

2 - Gratitude Activation (2 minutes)

Gratitude is the emotional frequency of fulfillment already realized. Speak aloud or silently three points of gratitude, mixing both present and future manifestations as though they have already arrived. This trains the field to recognize your vibration of "already done."

For example:
- "I am deeply grateful for the abundance that surrounds me."
- "I am grateful for the vibrant health pulsing through every cell."
- "I am grateful for the aligned partnerships unfolding with grace."

Gratitude bypasses resistance by assuming receipt. It stabilizes your frequency.

3 - Desire Visualization (5–7 minutes)

Here you enter the creative temple of Mind. Visualize your current desire as fully real:
- See the environment where it exists.
- Feel the emotions you experience living it.
- Observe the details with sensory richness: sights, sounds, smells, textures.

You are not daydreaming. You are broadcasting a vivid signal into the God Mind Field.

4 - Emotional Resonance Amplification (3–5 minutes)

Now, allow the emotional state of fulfillment to fully saturate your being.
- Feel the joy as though the manifestation already lives around you.
- Allow gratitude, peace, and certainty to flood your

body.
- Anchor this state as your new normal.

This step is not optional.
Emotion is the carrier wave that energizes the transmission.

5 - Certainty Declaration (1 minute)
Seal your transmission with spoken certainty:
- "It is done."
- "I am fully aligned with my highest timeline."
- "I allow the God Mind Field to orchestrate the perfect unfolding."

This declaration stabilizes your Permission Matrix and removes lingering doubt.

The Evening Calibration: Closing the Day's Field (5 minutes)

As the day completes, your final act is recalibration:
- Review your day without judgment.
- Identify any resistance, fear, or frustration that arose.
- Release each with simple acknowledgment:
  "I release all remaining static into the field for transmutation."
- Close with gratitude for both seen and unseen progress:
  "I trust the orchestration now underway."

The evening calibration ensures that your energetic broadcast remains clear through the night, where much dimensional processing occurs beyond conscious awareness.

This daily rhythm is your living laboratory.
Repetition is not redundancy — it is refinement.

Appendix B — The Belief Clearing Protocol: Rewriting the Permission Matrix

The God Mind Field does not respond to your surface affirmations.

It responds to your dominant energetic permissions. When your beliefs contradict your desires, the system receives mixed signals, delaying or distorting manifestation. Thus, belief reprogramming is the purification of your command structure.

Here is the complete method:

Step 1: Identification of the Limiting Belief
Begin with radical honesty. Articulate the belief clearly and specifically. Vague identification allows the belief to hide.

Example:
"Money is hard to earn."
"I am not worthy of true love."
"Health declines with age."

Bring the belief into the light of full language.

Step 2: Sourcing the Origin
Interrogate its genesis:
- Where did I learn this?
- Whose voice planted this belief?
- Is this belief my own, or inherited?

Have I personally tested its universal truth?
This step reveals that most limiting beliefs are adopted from family, culture, religion, or societal norms — not personal discovery.

Step 3: Challenging the Validity
Now you break its illusion through conscious reasoning:
- Is this belief universally true?
- Are there countless examples that disprove it?
- Does the God Mind Field operate by limitation or possibility?

The practitioner recognizes that all limiting beliefs collapse under full inspection.

Step 4: Writing the Aligned Truth
Craft the reprogramming statement — not as wishful thinking, but as present fact:
- "Wealth flows easily to me as I serve my highest work."
- "I am fully capable of receiving love that nourishes and uplifts."
- "My body regenerates in alignment with its divine blueprint."

This is the new coding of your Permission Matrix.

Step 5: Emotional Installation
Intellect alone cannot overwrite belief.

You must emotionally install the new program:
- Visualize yourself living fully inside the new belief.
- Feel the emotional reality of this truth already operating.
- Let gratitude flood your system for this upgraded permission.

Step 6: Repetition and Anchoring
Repetition stabilizes neural and energetic patterns.

Speak, write, or meditate on your new belief multiple times

daily for at least 21 days to install it as default operating code. Repetition is how the subconscious accepts new instructions.

Belief reprogramming is not a one-time event.
It is ongoing refinement as new desires emerge and deeper layers surface.

Appendix C — The God Mind Alignment Meditation: Daily Energetic Recalibration

This brief daily meditation allows you to continually align with the full architecture of manifestation, even amidst daily life pressures.

10-Minute Alignment Protocol
1- Centering (1 minute)
- Sit upright.
- Breathe deeply.
- Become fully present in your body.

2 - God Mind Connection (1 minute)
Silently declare:
"I am a Fractal Mind of the Infinite. The God Mind lives through me."

Feel the field envelop you.

3 - Desire Statement (1 minute)
Speak aloud or silently:
"I now create _____ (state desire) in perfect alignment with my soul path and Divine Will."

4 - Alignment Check (2 minutes)
Ask within:
"Does this desire serve my highest growth?"

"Is it free of fear, ego, or urgency?"

Listen for subtle affirmations or corrections.

5 - Emotional Charge (2 minutes)
- Generate deep gratitude as if fulfillment is already real.
- Anchor joy, peace, and certainty into your nervous system.

6 - Surrender Statement (1 minute)
Speak:
"I release resistance. I trust the orchestration of the Infinite Field."

7 - Radiant Seal (1 minute)
Visualize light radiating outward from your being — your signal now live within the God Mind Field.

This alignment can be done daily, or as needed when you feel static or misalignment arising.

Appendix D — The Resistance Release Exercise: Clearing Emotional Static

Emotional resistance is the energetic static that disrupts your broadcast. This exercise allows you to dissolve such static rather than suppress it.

The "Feel and Dissolve" Method
1 - Locate the Emotional Block
- Sit in stillness.
- Identify where in the body resistance resides — chest, stomach, throat, etc.

2 - Permission to Feel
- Allow the emotion full access without suppression.
- Let it fully express as intensity rises.
- Do not judge the feeling.

3 - Amplify Awareness
Ask:
"What message do you bring me?"
"What belief is hiding beneath you?"

Listen without resistance.

4 - Compassionate Acknowledgment
Speak internally:
"Thank you for protecting me. You are no longer required.
I release you."

5 - Breath Release
- Inhale deeply.
- Exhale while visualizing the emotional charge dissipating as vapor or light.

6 - Gratitude Seal
Close with:
"I am grateful for this release. My field is now clear."

Each release removes static and restores energetic coherence, amplifying manifestation precision.

Appendix E — The Master Alignment Audit

Use these self-inquiries to maintain ongoing coherence:
- Is my current desire fully aligned with my soul's evolutionary path?
- Is there any urgency, fear, or emotional attachment

beneath this desire?

- Am I seeking to control, or am I allowing perfect orchestration?
- Am I emotionally embodying the outcome as though already fulfilled?
- Is my belief system fully permitting this reality?
- Have I surrendered the timing to dimensional processing?

When all responses are clean, you are transmitting a fully coherent signal.

Appendix F — The God Mind Practitioner's Creed

This creed is not a mantra for temporary encouragement.
It is the living code of your identity as a God Mind Practitioner.

I am Mind.
I am Creator.
I am a Fractal of the Infinite God Mind.
I create with clarity, alignment, and love.
I release resistance and allow the field to organize reality perfectly.
I serve my own evolution and the evolution of the Whole.
I am responsible for my creations.
I manifest in harmony with my soul path and Divine Will.
I trust the unfolding.
I receive with gratitude.
I am, now and always, a conscious practitioner of the God Mind Principle.

Bibliography

Primary Sources & Influences

1. The Kybalion — Three Initiates (1912)
The foundational Hermetic text outlining the Seven Hermetic Principles, including Mentalism: "All is Mind."
2. **The Emerald Tablet of Hermes Trismegistus — Translations by various scholars**
The ancient Hermetic maxim "As above, so below; as within, so without" central to manifestation mechanics.
3. **The Tao Te Ching — Lao Tzu (6th Century BCE)**
Timeless teachings on alignment, surrender, and non-resistance as paths to flow with universal intelligence.
4. **The Bhagavad Gita — Translations by Eknath Easwaran, Swami Prabhupada, others**
Insights into desireless action, soul alignment, and dharma.
5. The Bible: King James Version — Genesis, Proverbs, **Gospels**
Mystical layers of creation, intention, and alignment: "As a man thinketh in his heart, so is he."
6. **A Course in Miracles — Helen Schucman (1976)**
Explores perception, projection, and the role of Mind in generating reality.
7. **The Power of Now — Eckhart Tolle (1997)**
On presence, non-resistance, and surrender as access points to the field of creation.
8. **The Law of Attraction — Esther & Jerry Hicks (2006)**
Modern articulation of vibrational manifestation through Abraham teachings.
9. **The Biology of Belief — Bruce H. Lipton, PhD (2005)**
Scientific explanation of how belief and perception

influence biological reality.

10.   Breaking the Habit of Being Yourself — Dr. Joe Dispenza (2012)
Advanced neuroscience and quantum theory applications in reprogramming the mind-body field.

11.   The Holographic Universe — Michael Talbot (1991)
Explores reality as a holographic projection governed by consciousness.

12.   The Field: The Quest for the Secret Force of the Universe — Lynne McTaggart (2001)
Scientific research on zero-point field theory and intention-based manifestation.

13.   Power vs. Force — Dr. David R. Hawkins (1995)
Calibrated scale of consciousness levels, vibrational fields, and emotional frequencies.

14.   Reality Transurfing (Vols. 1–5) — Vadim Zeland (2004–2008)
Comprehensive model of how intention, energy, and vibrational states create alternate life tracks.

15.   Man's Search for Meaning — Viktor Frankl (1946)
Examines the human role in choosing meaning and perception even under extreme conditions.

Annotated Reference List
(With Brief Commentary)

The Kybalion — Three Initiates
Provides the original formulation of the "All is Mind" principle foundational to this work.

The Emerald Tablet
The esoteric axiom "As within, so without" serves as the operating model for manifestation mechanics.

The Tao Te Ching — Lao Tzu
A poetic exploration of non-resistance, surrender, and alignment with the Tao (universal field).

The Bhagavad Gita
A complete dialogue on divine will, non-attachment to outcomes, and action aligned with purpose.

The Bible (Proverbs & Gospels)
Wisdom on thought, faith, and the creative role of Mind as a reflection of divine nature.

A Course in Miracles
Illuminates how perception governs personal and collective reality, offering tools for purification of belief.

The Power of Now — Eckhart Tolle
Anchors the reader into presence, where manifestation power is most active.

The Law of Attraction — Abraham-Hicks
Provides accessible teachings on vibrational alignment, desire, and receiving.

The Biology of Belief — Dr. Bruce Lipton
Bridges science and spirituality, showing the physical impact of belief on biology.

Breaking the Habit of Being Yourself — Dr. Joe Dispenza
Offers neuroscientific processes to rewire neural circuits and emotional imprints.

The Holographic Universe — Michael Talbot
Proposes reality as an informational projection shaped by Mind, mirroring Hermetic thought.

The Field — Lynne McTaggart
Scientific exploration of intention, quantum fields, and collective consciousness research.

Power vs. Force — Dr. David Hawkins
Calibrates vibrational levels of consciousness, correlating to manifestation acceleration.

Reality Transurfing — Vadim Zeland
Introduces highly detailed mechanics of shifting life tracks through vibrational tuning and non-resistance.

Man's Search for Meaning — Viktor Frankl
Demonstrates the inviolable creative power of human choice even under external oppression.

Further Reading for the Initiate

For readers who wish to continue their journey deeper into God Mind mastery, spiritual anthropology, and applied consciousness, the following works are highly recommended:

- The Untethered Soul — Michael A. Singer
- Becoming Supernatural — Dr. Joe Dispenza
- Letting Go: The Pathway of Surrender — Dr. David R. Hawkins
- The Surrender Experiment — Michael A. Singer
- Seat of the Soul — Gary Zukav
- Your Sacred Self — Dr. Wayne Dyer
- Autobiography of a Yogi — Paramahansa Yogananda
- The Tao of Physics — Fritjof Capra
- Dying To Be Me — Anita Moorjani
- The Cosmic Doctrine — Dion Fortune
- The Secret Teachings of All Ages — Manly P. Hall
- Initiation — Elisabeth Haich

www.ingramcontent.com/pod-product-compliance
Lightning Source LLC
Chambersburg PA
CBHW071227090426
42736CB00014B/2998